THE SERBIAN EPIC

To Jeanne

Из љубави књигу посвећујем
Срцу моме, госпођи предрагој.

I dedicate this book, with love, to her
Who is my heart's delight, a lady dear.

THE SERBIAN EPIC BALLADS

AN ANTHOLOGY

Translated by
GEOFFREY N. W. LOCKE

With a Foreword by Muriel Heppell

ASWA

First published in a dual-language edition by Nolit, Belgrade, 1997
This edition enlarged and revised, published in 2002 by *A S WA*
(The Association of Serbian Writers Abroad)
PO Box 20772
London E3 5WF

Copyright © G.N.W. Locke 2002
Foreword © Muriel Heppell 2002

All rights reserved. No part of this work may be reproduced, stored
in a retrieval system, or transmitted in any form or by any means,
electronic, electrostatic, magnetic tape, mechanical, photocopying,
recording or otherwise, without the prior permission in writing of
the publisher.

ISBN 0-9541777-2-X

CONTENTS

ACKNOWLEDGMENTS *vii*

FOREWORD *ix*

INTRODUCTION *xii*

NOTES ON TRANSLITERATION AND PRONUNCIATION *xxxvii*

THE EPIC BALLADS:

Of the Mediaeval Empire

1. Tsar Dushan's Wedding 2
2. Saint Peter and his Mother 22
3. The Building of Ravanitsa 23
4. Banovich Strahinya 30

Of the Battle of Kosovo

5. Tsar Lazar and Tsaritsa Militsa 56
6. Stefan Musich 62
7. The Maiden of Kosovo 67
8. The Death of the Mother of the Yugovichi 72

Of Marko Kralyevich

9. Marko's First Heroic Deed 78
10. Marko drinks Wine during Ramadan 81
11. The Ploughing of Marko Kralyevich 84
12. How Marko went Hunting with the Turks 85
13. Marko Kralyevich and Musa the Highwayman 89
14. Marko Kralyevich and the Eagle 98
15. How the Turks came to Marko's Slava 100
16. The Death of Marko Kralyevich 105

Of the Outlaws

17. How Miyat Tomich became an Outlaw *112*
18. Starina Novak and Bold Radivoye *117*
19. Starina Novak and Knez Bogosav *121*
20. Old Vuyadin *124*
21. Mali Radoyitsa *126*

Of the Noblemen

22. The Death of Voivoda Priyezda *134*
23. How the Brothers Yakshich shared their Inheritance *138*
24. Ailing Doichin *142*
25. The Ban of Zrin and the Maiden Begzada *151*

Of the Border Raiders

26. Ivo Senkovich and the Aga of Ribnik *164*
27. Tadia Senyanin *176*

Of the Montenegrins

28. The Three Prisoners *184*
29. How they took Beg Lyubovich's Sheep *188*

Of the Nineteenth-Century Uprisings

30. The Start of the Revolt against the Dahiyas *194*

APPENDIX – NOTES ON THE BALLADS 213

ACKNOWLEDGMENTS

I acknowledge with affectionate gratitude the encouragement of my wife Jeanne, of my daughters Susan, Jane, and Catherine, and of my sister Heather, who jointly and severally pressed me into making this book. I had originally translated these poems piecemeal, over many years, purely for my own satisfaction and without thought of publication. All were done directly from the original Serbian, without reference to, or sight of, any other translations.

I am deeply grateful to Dr Leofranc Holford-Strevens of Oxford for having generously given of his enthusiasm and formidable scholarship in assisting with the original Introduction and Appendix of Notes to the first (dual-language) edition, containing twenty-five ballads, which was published by Nolit, Belgrade, in 1997, to mark the 75th anniversary of that Publishing House's foundation. In the course of revision and preparation for that edition I also received many constructive suggestions and much essential advice, both as to nuances of meaning in the original texts and as to historical and literary detail, from the editor of Nolit, the late lamented Mr Slobodan Djordjević, and from Dr Nada Milošević-Djordjević, Resident Professor of National Literature at Belgrade University, who also contributed the Foreword. I greatly valued both the sternness of their erudite criticism and the warmth of their friendship.

This second (single-language) edition contains five additional ballads, and the whole book has been extensively revised. A number of flaws, errors, and a few mistranslations which regrettably survived into the first edition, have been amended and corrected. I am deeply grateful to Mr Dušan Puvačić, Lecturer of London University and editor of ASWA, for his invaluable advice and assistance in all of this. If faults remain, I am responsible.

I wish also to express my gratitude to Dr Muriel Heppell of London University for so kindly contributing the Foreword to this edition.

The original texts were taken from the following two scholastic anthologies, which contain useful notes on the many unusual and archaic expressions which are found in the language of the Serbian Epics: *Epske Narodne Pjesme,* Ed. Čubelić (Školska Knjiga, Zagreb, 1951), and *Narodne Junačke Pesme o Marku Kraljeviću,* Ed. Djurić (Znanje, Beograd, 1953). Much additional material in the Notes to this edition derives from the excellent reference book *Narodna Književnost*, by Pešić & Milošević-Djordjević (Trebnik, Beograd, 1996).

G.N.W.L.

FOREWORD

*by Dr Muriel Heppell,
Emeritus Reader in the Medieval History of
Orthodox Eastern Europe, University of London*

During the relatively short period of its full existence (from the coronation of King Stephen the First in 1202 to the battle of Kosovo in 1389), the medieval kingdom of Serbia showed a remarkable degree of creativity in various fields. Perhaps the expression of this best known in the western world is the large number of small, mainly monastic churches, outstanding both for their architectural form and their exquisite fresco paintings. Though much of this has been damaged through centuries of neglect, and the depredations of alien invaders, enough remains for its quality to be appreciated by experts from many nations. Less well known, except to professional historians, are the written Lives of rulers and church leaders, in which the authors adapted the traditional formalised *vita*, or saint's life, to something approaching the modern concept of biography. The same is true of the comprehensive legal code, or *Zakonik*, first promulgated by Tsar Dušan in 1349; this certainly deserves more attention than it has so far received from western historians.

Not least among the achievements of this small kingdom was the large volume of orally transmitted epic and ballad poetry which it produced, and continued to produce after the fall of the kingdom and the dispersion into exile of much of its population, right up to the beginning of the 19th century. Much of this relates to historical events and personages, but these poems present history seen through the prism of poetic imagination, which gives it an extra dimension, and one which academic historians are too prone to undervalue. These poems, recited by itinerant bards, did much to keep alive the nation's memories of its past, and its sense of identity, during the centuries of Ottoman rule.

It was not until the first half of the 19th century that a large selection of these poems was collected and published, thanks to the energy and determination of the Serbian philologist Vuk Karadžić (1787-1864). They were soon translated into German, and their literary quality was immediately recognised by a number of German writers and critics, notably Jacob Grimm and Goethe. Translations into other languages (including English) followed, and since that time these poems have assumed their rightful place as part of the heritage of European literature.

Translating these poems into English presents technical as well as artistic difficulties, because of the different structure of the two languages. In this new translation of a selection of the Serbian poems, Geoffrey Locke has very effectively used the traditional pentameter of English blank verse. The translations are preceded by a scholarly and comprehensive Introduction which provides a sufficiently detailed historical and literary background for the poems. This is necessary if they are to be fully appreciated by modern readers, since many of them were composed some centuries ago and reflect a world very different from out own.

In the Foreword to the first (bi-lingual) edition of this book, published in Belgrade in 1997, Dr Nada Milošević-Djordjević, Professor of National Literature in the University of Belgrade, pays a remarkable tribute to the literary quality and worth of Geoffrey Locke's work. She says: "These translations are a work of art in themselves, whilst accurately preserving the sense and meaning of the originals. Mr Locke has succeeded admirably in his aim of presenting a selection of ballads covering a wide historical range, in displaying the richness of Serbian epic poetry, and in making clear how the process of composition, memorisation, development, and repetition were both a catharsis and a special source of strength and resolve to the Serbian people. He most skilfully, and with exceptional poetic sensibility, reflects the differences between the style of description, for instance, in tales of single combat from ancient times and that in tales of later ages. In the lyrical parts he preserves the special characteristics of emotional stylisation found in the originals. His settings have all the sheen of old silver, even its patina. One has the strong impression that one is not in fact reading a translation, but that one is enjoying an entertaining, international, and universal work of art – a song sung in its mother-tongue." She goes on to say that his translations "not only conjure up the impression of a bygone civilization, but also give it permanent relevance."

It is to be hoped that this English edition will win for both the mostly anonymous poets and their interpreter the appreciation they deserve.

M.H.
London, 2002

INTRODUCTION

The Serbian Epic Ballads are unique, and constitute the richest oral epic material in any single European language. Their value and appeal derive from the fact that, so far from being mere artificial recitation of obscure and half-forgotten tales of bygone ages (as is so much of the 'folklore' of most other European cultures, including the English) they are, on the contrary, the product of a continuous living tradition extending over the last several centuries. In its evolved form, this oral poetry's standard of artistic expression, balance, and content is so high that it is justifiably taken as a principal basis for the serious proposition that the early Greek epics, including the Iliad and the Odyssey, were likewise the product of an entirely oral tradition, and that Homer was the recorder, rather than the original author of the works attributed to him. It has the additional characteristic, possibly less interesting to strict academics, of being mostly very entertaining and frequently laced with humour.

These are not literal, word-for-word translations. I have throughout sought to convey the true sense and meaning of the originals passage by passage, and to set them in a form of English verse appropriate to their nature and style and in particular their musicality, bearing in mind that the original ballads were designed to be sung or spoken, not read. I am well aware of the near-impossibility of transcribing poetry satisfactorily from one language to another (for the poetry of each has its own peculiar magic), but have endeavoured to make workmanlike black-and-white reproductions of originals which glow with colour.

Although it is perfectly possible to enjoy these ballads for their own sake, since as literature they are timeless, for a greater appreciation of them it is helpful to know the outline of the historical background which they reflect and out of which they grew, so as to be able to understand how they came into existence and flourished for so long a period. It is also desirable to know something of the bards who composed and performed them, and to be aware of the characteristics of the Serbian language so as to appreciate not only the rhythms and cadences of its epic verse but also the artistic mastery which those bards had to possess in order to achieve, within the severely stylised form which tradition demanded, the superb flow of narrative and depths of poetic insight which characterise their ballads.

These matters are summarised in the following sections under four headings:

(1) The historical background.
(2) The bards, and the oral tradition.
(3) The Serbian language, and the prosody of the epic ballads.
(4) Notes on translation.

1

THE HISTORICAL BACKGROUND

Of all the tribes that took part in the migrations into Europe from the east during the Dark Ages, the Serbs, a Slavonic people, and the Bulgars (who claim a Tartar origin) were those who went the farthest south. By the seventh century A.D. the Serbs had settled into the south-western part of the Balkan peninsula, whilst the Bulgars occupied the south-eastern part, in heartlands the boundaries of which differed little from those of today. When these pagans arrived in the southern Balkans they came initially into conflict with, but eventually under the strong cultural and religious influence of Constantinople, then the citadel of the Byzantine Emperor, the centre of the Christian Eastern Orthodox Church, and a last bastion of European civilization after the fall of Rome. By the ninth century the two Greek missionaries Saints Cyril and Methodius, and their disciples, had not only converted the Serbs and Bulgars to Christianity but had also translated the Gospels and the Orthodox liturgy into their language and had constructed for them the Glagolitic and Cyrillic alphabets, based on the Greek but admirably adapted to suit the very different Slavonic speech-patterns. (The Bulgars eventually abandoned their original language: they speak a Slavonic dialect similar to Serbian). The Glagolitic alphabet has now fallen into disuse, but the Cyrillic, later adopted by the Russians when they were evangelized, is still in normal use today in Serbia and Bulgaria. The Croats, who had migrated into the Balkans at about the same time as the Serbs, and who effectively share their language with them, had meanwhile remained in the north-western part of the region and there came wholly under the influence of the Roman church. Looking to central Europe, their culture and history developed, for that and other reasons, in a very different way from that of the Serbs.

It is interesting that, from the earliest times, their neighbours in the Balkans had observed that the Serbs were much given to singing ballads about all manner of subjects, not only epic, both in the courts of the nobility and in the towns and villages, and that their bards were especially honoured and respected. The tradition was therefore in place well before the devastating events of the Middle Ages plunged the Serbs into a long period of isolation and foreign occupation and oppression, which they endured bereft of all but their pride and of the songs in which they expressed it.

By the second half of the fourteenth century, therefore, the Serbs had been well established for some seven hundred years in that south-western part of the Balkan peninsula which is still their home. There was, of course, plenty of turbulence, with clan fighting clan and intermittent warfare with neighbouring nations: in this Serbia differed little from the rest of mediaeval Europe, but this was for the Serbs their great era of power and prosperity. They had grown into a minor empire extending from the Danube at Belgrade to the Adriatic at Dubrovnik (Ragusa) and southwards into most of the Greek peninsula. Their chieftains now called themselves kings, and the strongest of them was proclaimed as an emperor (although they continued to pay nominal homage to the 'real' Byzantine Emperor in Constantinople). There were, however, no long-lasting dynasties. The Serbs have always been an obstinate and strongly individualistic people, with a marked sense of their own worth: rather yeomen than serfs, the mediaeval Serbs were willing to obey and serve only those whom they respected as individuals. Consequently, upon the death of a monarch it by no means necessarily followed that his son or designated heir would succeed. The integrity of the nation was assured by the formidable prowess of its warriors, which had been proved many times. Its prosperity was based upon abundant agricultural production, upon the commerce generated by its position on the land route between Europe and Asia Minor, and upon the exploitation of minerals, in particular silver, which was exported in great quantities, and gold. A combination of religious faith and the desire to be remembered led successive kings and princes to undertake many public works. As well as roads and bridges, they built churches and monasteries which were sumptuously decorated and embellished: the architecture and fresco paintings of many of them were of such high artistic standards as to equal anything in pre-Renaissance Europe. There was a developing literature, and the Serbs were famous for their musical accomplishments, at the forefront of which was the singing of ballads by professional bards. The climax was the reign of Tsar Stefan Dushan the Great (1331–55). Particularly noteworthy was his introduction of a code of law which was in advance of any obtaining in most of the rest of mediaeval Europe. However, after his death there was bitter feuding over the succession, and the coherence of the State was weakened.

The time for such self-indulgence was ill-chosen. Looming near, in the east, was the menace of militant Islam. The nature of the pressure from the east differed from that of the Islamic blitzkrieg into western Europe which had earlier swept the Moors to within a hundred miles of Paris, and which had left large parts of Spain under Islamic rule. It was not until the eleventh century that the Turks, originally a tribe of nomadic horsemen from Central Asia which had occupied the Anatolian peninsula and embraced Islam, embarked upon a determined campaign of empire-building by conquest, initially towards the east. They quickly earned a reputation as formidable warriors who firmly held that which they had conquered.

At the beginning of the fourteenth century the 'Osmanli', or 'Ottomans' were the dominant group of the western Turks, and in 1345 they crossed the Dardanelles into Europe (ironically, at the invitation of the then Byzantine Emperor, who required temporary military assistance in a dynastic feud). Seizing this opportunity for expansion to the west, and bypassing the still-impregnable citadel that was Constantinople, the Ottoman Turks were by the year of Tsar Dushan's death well established in Gallipoli and were regularly conducting raids in force into the Balkans (whilst at the other end of Europe the English and French had embarked upon a hundred years of war, and Crecy had already been fought). In 1371 the Serbs and Bulgars engaged the Ottoman Turks at the Battle of the Maritsa River and suffered defeat. By 1389 the Turks had occupied Bulgaria and parts of southern Serbia, and in that year (twenty-six years before Agincourt), the Serbian Tsar Lazar put the matter to the test. The unity of his empire was shaky, the reliability of his allies and of his subordinate kings and commanders variable. He faced a large disciplined Ottoman army under Sultan Murat and on St Vitus' Day (*Vidovdan* – 15th June by the Julian calendar still used by the Orthodox Church, but observed on the 28th by the modern Gregorian calendar) he engaged it in pitched battle at Kosovo and was defeated. It is clear that both sides were conscious that they were fighting for their Faiths, and the ferocity of the battle can be gauged from the fact that the Commanders-in-Chief of both armies, Lazar and Murat, were killed and the casualties were heavy on both sides. It has been reasonably argued that, in historical and strategic terms, it was Maritsa (1371), and not Kosovo, that was the decisive battle. Be that as it may, the Serbian percep-

INTRODUCTION

tion was that it was at Kosovo that they had thrown everything they had into the balance, and that it was there that the flower of their chivalry and manhood had sacrificed itself in a final effort to defend the nation from slavery and Europe from Islamic domination. Although their last fortress (Smederevo) did not fall until 1459, they saw that before Kosovo they had been an independent and justifiably proud kingdom: after it nothing could halt their decline into vassaldom under a foreign and heathen occupier, stripped of their wealth and dignity, but never their pride.

The Turkish tide moved slowly but inexorably northward and onward into Europe. In 1453 Constantinople fell at last, and the last Byzantine Emperor was killed within its walls. The great city now became, as Istanbul, the seat of the Sultan and the capital of the Ottoman empire. In 1526 the Hungarians were heavily defeated and their country subjugated. Three years later the Turks reached Vienna and they were there, for the first time, checked, but the menace remained and grew. In 1689 Vienna was once again besieged by a determined Turkish army. This time the Turks were decisively defeated and finally repulsed. The Ottoman empire was now at the zenith of its expansion. In Europe, besides the Balkans and Greece, it included Hungary and Romania. In Asia it embraced Turkey and the Middle East as far as the Caspian Sea and the Persian Gulf. The Levant, Egypt, and the Mediterranean coast to Tripolitania were all Ottoman provinces. In the Balkans a frontier zone where the Ottoman and Austrian empires met became established between Croatia and the territory known as Bosnia. This frontier zone was called the Krajina (pronounced 'Krayina' – see Notes on Transliteration and Pronunciation at page xxxvii), which simply means 'Borderland', a name sharing its Slavonic root with 'Ukraine'. The western side of the Bosnian territory is practically cut off from the Adriatic by the great mountain ranges which rise steeply out of the sea along most of its length and through which there are few practical passes. The narrow coastal strip (Dalmatia) was dominated by Venetian strongholds, and thus formed the western Ottoman frontier.

Serbia, Bosnia, and all but an enclave of Montenegro were now Turkish provinces, surrounded and isolated. Bosnia itself, with its southern province of Hercegovina, was a territory which had not formed part of Serbia proper, as had Montenegro, but was populated largely by Orthodox Slavs. It appears that there had never been any serious compulsion to form a lasting Bosnian state, and that the region lacked sufficient natural advantages to induce any of its frequent invaders to establish one. The population lived mostly in scattered patriarchal communities, and although they were all Christians it seems that the clergy became ineffective, resulting in the rise of an apparently benign heresy similar to that of the Cathars of southern France, the adherents to which were called 'Bogomils'. Now, however, in strategic terms Bosnia had been thrust into prominence by becoming the Ottoman empire's vulnerable North-west Frontier Province, abutting as it did the two powerful and hostile Christian empires of Austria and Venice. The Turks could obviously permit no laxity in the internal security of so sensitive a region. This is probably the reason why in Bosnia, unlike in most parts of the Ottoman empire where Christians, though disdained, were tolerated, pressure was brought to bear on the indigenous inhabitants to demonstrate total loyalty to their Turkish masters by converting to Islam. Various explanations have been put forward as to why some of the Serbian inhabitants of Bosnia, mainly landowners and town-dwellers, succumbed, whilst the Serbs of Montenegro and of Serbia proper did not. The most likely reason is that the Bosnians, never having formed a recognizable nation, lacked any focus of identity, and were without significant historical traditions or institutions, whether political or religious. At all events, many of them committed apostasy and started to identify themselves wholly with the Turkish regime and culture (but not its language). In the eyes of the true Serbs they literally "became Turks" *(poturice)* and, whereas the Serbs' hatred of the real Turks was tempered by respect for their military and administrative abilities, for these *collaborateurs* they felt nothing but contempt. The con-

INTRODUCTION

sequences of their recreancy reverberate to this day for, in the manner of converts, many subsequently outdid the Turks themselves in the oppression of those who, despite persecution, remained steadfastly faithful to their religion and their traditions, and among the Balkan peoples memories are very long. The Bogomils disappeared: one theory is that they constituted a majority of the converts to Islam. At all events, after the Ottoman conquest Bosnia and Hercegovina (especially the latter) became regions in which the Serbian epic ballads were particularly intensely and widely cultivated. Many of the greatest bards came from there, and Bosnian places and personalities appear in many of the tales. It is also significant that even the Bosnian converts to Islam continued to compose and sing epic ballads in the Serbian language and in the traditional Serbian form, albeit with a different cast of heroes.

The Croats and Slovenes, meanwhile, were content to be absorbed into Roman Catholic Austria as minor provinces. However, the southern part of the Croatian territory was the Krajina – the 'Borderland' – and this vulnerable region had to be secured. To perform the arduous and dangerous task of holding the Imperial frontier against the Ottoman empire, the Austrians invited Serbs escaping from dispossession and persecution at the hands of the Turks (and, in Bosnia, of their recreant brothers as well), to occupy the Krajina and do the job for them in return for land rights and security. This "Militärgrenze" was not politically or administratively part of Croatia, but was commanded and controlled directly by Vienna through a headquarters at Karlovac. The expatriate Serbs defended it so successfully that this frontier was never significantly breached in the course of several centuries, and their descendants remained there until all of them (some half-a-million) were forcibly expelled by the newly-independent Croats in 1995 during the Yugoslavian civil war.

The reaction of the true Serbs to the Ottoman conquest was characteristic of them. Although stunned by the catastrophe that had overtaken them, these obstinate and individualistic people grimly resolved to resist indefinitely the occupation of their country by any means available to them. With no hope of effective external assistance, the Serbs of Serbia and Montenegro, and those in Bosnia who had spurned apostasy (at least half the population) defied all rational logic by refusing to accept that their defeat was final and their lowly place in the massive Ottoman empire permanent.

The terrain favoured them. The wooded mountains with narrow winding passes which cover much of the region make ideal guerrilla country for those with the will and courage to exploit them. Some formed themselves into organized bands of outlaws – 'haiduks' *(hajduci)* – whose main occupation was robbery and pillage. As, however, the only people worth robbing were the Turks or their Bosnian collaborators, the haiduks were generally admired and supported by the ordinary people. Some who had become exiled, particularly to the Dalmatian coast, operated as border raiders called 'uskoks' *(uskoci)*, frequently as Venetian irregulars. Many, with perhaps more honourable motives, grouped themselves into companies – 'chete' *(čete)*, hence 'chetniks' – and concerned themselves with harassing the Turkish lines of communication, attacking any slackly defended outposts, and generally denying the Turks full security and enjoyment of their occupation. The Montenegrin Serbs, in particular, were so successful in these activities, supported by an implacable determination on the part of the entire population to reject Turkish rule whatever the price in blood, that their craggy land was never totally subdued or brought under permanent occupation. Indeed, at the end of the eighteenth century the then ruling Vladika (Prince-Bishop) of Montenegro was able to obtain a formal admission from the Sultan that the Montenegrins "had never been subjects of the Sublime Porte."

It must be said that Ottoman Turkish rule was, at times, not unduly oppressive for those who did not oppose it. The Christian religion was tolerated, and for considerable periods local chieftains were accorded wide administrative powers under their

INTRODUCTION

Turkish overlords, and would even campaign with them as mercenaries, but eventually some local injustice, excessive taxation, or a run of successes by guerrilla bands would revive the bitter memory of Kosovo and fan the ever-smouldering embers of revolt. Such outbursts were put down and punished with terrible severity. Whole communities would be annihilated or dispersed, and the public execution of individuals by impalement was commonplace well into the nineteenth century. Despite all these horrors, and despite the knowledge that by compliance they might avoid them, the Serbs persisted in their sporadic but incessant resistance, generation after generation, for nearly four hundred years. It is obvious that only an exceptionally robust people, with a strong sense of identity even in diaspora, and with a powerful cultural tradition based on strong religious faith, could have sustained such behaviour for so long: their epic ballads undoubtedly played a major part in maintaining as well as reflecting their courage and endurance. It is, indeed, arguable that devotion to the tradition of balladising is as marked a defining characteristic of the widely-dispersed Serbian nation as is their Orthodox religion.

By the end of the eighteenth century the Ottoman Empire was clearly in decline. In outlying provinces such as Serbia local satraps were becoming dangerously independent, and were imposing impossible burdens of tax and forced labour on the native population. The degree of oppression had become such that much of Serbia proper was severely depopulated, huge numbers having fled to neighbouring Austro-Hungarian lands where, nevertheless, they clung fiercely to their identity and their pride, and expressed both constantly in their epic ballads. In 1804 came the First Serbian Uprising. Haiduks and chetniks, all experienced guerrillas, combined with the hardy peasants to form an organized army under Karageorge, and inflicted several significant defeats upon the Turkish army before being themselves finally defeated in 1813. Terrible punitive measures ensued, forcing large-scale movements of refugees. The savagery of these reprisals may be judged by the nature of the war memorial which the Turks chose to erect on the road from Niš to Pirot, in Eastern Serbia – it takes the form of a tower constructed of Serbian skulls. The Second Uprising took place in 1815, led by Miloš Obrenović, and although not immediately successful, it led to escalating military and diplomatic efforts which finally enabled Serbia, by the 1878 Treaty of Berlin, to be formally recognised once again as the free and independent Kingdom that it had previously been. Rapid modernisation, and in particular the spread of literacy, meant that the traditional living bards no longer had a place at the centre of popular culture, with the result that they and their skills inevitably faded away.

However, their unique heritage of superb national poetry which, upon its being recorded and published (as described in Section Two) had aroused the admiration of such European literary giants as Herder, Goethe, Jakob Grimm, and Pushkin, remained for the Serbs a source of justifiable pride and a fundamental basis of literature and education thereafter. This continued into the ensuing turbulent twentieth century, during most of which the Serbian and Montenegrin nations subordinated their hard-won independence in the interests of the wider state of Yugoslavia. The dissolution of that State by way of a tragic civil war in the last decade of the twentieth century was accompanied by a barrage of anti-Serbian propaganda and misrepresentation of unprecedented ferocity and mendacity. As part of this campaign of blanket denigration it was asserted that the Serbian Epics were, firstly, no more than an artificial construction of nineteenth-century intellectuals and, secondly, that by encouraging an unhealthy preoccupation with an ancient lost battle, together with xenophobic incitement to violence, they were material which unscrupulous politicians could and did use to "manipulate" the Serbian people into aggression (for the first time, be it noted, in their long history).

The first proposition is quite untenable: the facts are as summarised by Jakob Grimm as early as 1823: "These Serbian songs are not the result of laborious research in old manuscripts, but have all been recorded from the living voice of the people …

INTRODUCTION

[they] provide much-needed and substantial material for the study of epic poetry." The second assertion, that the Epics constitute inflammatory material for rabble-rousing, simply does not survive examination. Even a cursory reading of this representative anthology will reveal that the material in question in no way lends itself to the whipping up of self-pity, bloodlust, or vengeance, nor does it contain any trace of incitement to hatred of foreigners (except, for obvious reasons, the Ottoman Turks – themselves now a relic of history). It will be seen that the Serbian epics celebrate no posturing demi-gods, no Valkyres, and no Valhalla; there is no bombast in them, and no glorification of war – on the contrary, they honour only courage and fortitude in adversity. The 'Kosovo' cycle of ballads, which forms only a small if important part of the whole, is characterised by sadness, respect for the fallen, and full recognition of the tragedy of war. It should also be remembered that Kosovo was a purely defensive battle, not one in which the Serbs were attempting to impose their hegemony on others – a Dunkirk, perhaps, rather than an Austerlitz.

It may well be true that their great Epics helped to inspire the Serbs (or "manipulate" them, if that term is preferred) to undertake their apparently hopeless and horribly dangerous bid to challenge the still-mighty Ottoman empire in open, rather than guerrilla warfare, in their Uprisings of 1804–13 and 1815. The situation at the end of the twentieth century, however, was totally different: no meaningful comparison can be drawn.

It may be seen from this very brief summary that the history of the Serbian nation from the fourteenth to the nineteenth centuries, which is the period covered by the classic epic ballads, falls into four main phases – the mediaeval Empire, its downfall at the Battle of Kosovo, the centuries of dogged resistance to vassaldom and, finally, the battles for renewed independence in the nineteenth century. It is a remarkable and heroic story, fit to be recorded and reflected in epic verse: that is exactly what happened.

The Serbs by R.G.D. Laffan (Dorset Press, New York, 1989), gives a more detailed account of the history of Serbia, whilst

A Short History of the Yugoslav Peoples by F. Singleton (Cambridge, 1985) sets the story into the broader context. An interesting view from 'the other side of the hill' is found in *The Decline and Fall of the Ottoman Empire,* by A. Palmer (Murray, 1992).

2

THE SERBIAN BARDS AND THE ORAL TRADITION

The practice of ballad singing is an integral part of Serbian culture. There are reports of it as early as the seventh century, and by mediaeval times the fame of the Serbian bards, and recognition of the special content and style of their work, had spread well beyond their borders. Their emblem and 'trademark' was the *gusle*, a single-stringed fiddle, preferably made of maple wood and elaborately carved, with which they usually accompanied themselves when singing their ballads

These illiterate bards (who were both men and women, many blind) did not confine their repertoire to songs of battles long ago, but sang of recent and contemporary personalities and events, for they were composers and improvisers as well as performers. Travelling between courts, towns, and villages, they provided news, comment, and entertainment much as the radio and television do today. (It would be wrong to take the analogy too far: their work was not mere journalism, but deliberately cultivated artistic expression within a highly disciplined stylistic convention). In the centuries of Turkish occupation the Serbian bard, by using every artifice of declamation, gesture, and musical expression, would bring alive the tales of Serbia's former grandeur, of the leaden crash of Kosovo, and of the exploits of greater and lesser heroes of the recent as well as the remoter past. The bard had no need to set the background for tales of heroism amid misfortune: the misfortune was all around them, and there would be few in his or her audience, often in exile, who had not themselves been directly affected by the harsh reality of constant conflict against the occupiers of their country, and who had not lost their homes, relatives, or friends in such conflict or in the bloody reprisals which inevitably followed. When the bard sang of heroism they knew what it really meant: they had no romantic illusions about it and would detect, and reject, any recitation of mere bombast. To such people, with their long artistic traditions, a ballad had to be convincing, sincere, and of the highest standard of poetic merit if it were not to ring hollow, and when it did meet these requirements it became an instrument of catharsis and a powerful source of inspiration and resolve. This interaction between artist and audience ensured that those ballads which were able to stand the test of time achieved that remarkable characteristic of authority which is the hallmark of all great art.

The ballads would undergo constant repetition, being initially improvised but then varied, amended, and polished by successive generations of bards, and in this way a process of refining and "honing" took place, with the selection of the best being determined by that most ruthless of all forms of artistic judgement – a knowledgeable and appreciative but critical audience. That European literature is now fortunate enough to possess a large published body of authentic Serbian epic ballads is almost entirely due to the work of one man, the great Serbian philologist **Vuk Stefanović Karadžić** (1787–1864) who, in the first four decades of the nineteenth century dedicated himself to collecting and recording them as they then stood. Between 1813 and 1841 he and his assistants travelled extensively in Serbia and in the lands of the Serbian diaspora, collecting ballads and publishing them in successive groups (in Vienna and Leipzig). In all, there are over a thousand poems in those published collections, and about another two thousand which were not published. The majority of the ballads in this selection are derived from those published collections. Karadžić defined two main categories of Serbian oral poetry, the so-called 'men's songs' which were largely concerned with battles, single combat, and heroic deeds (epics, in the true sense), and 'women's songs', which dealt with matters of everyday life and love, festivals, and suchlike topics, whilst recognizing that there were some with the characteristics of both. (Scholars tend to reserve the term 'ballad' for the women's songs. Since, however, the English word 'ballad' as precisely describes the epic songs, I have ignored this distinction).

It is doubly fortunate that Vuk Karadžić conducted his operations at that particular moment in history. Firstly, the practice of ballad singing was then still flourishing: the Serbs were exhilarated by their success, albeit partial, in the First and Second Uprisings which, true to form, they celebrated in newly-composed epic ballads. Secondly, Karadžić was operating just before the dawn of universal literacy in Europe – a general blessing, but one which inevitably led to the disappearance of the bard as the sole purveyor of oral entertainment, historical narrative, and news, and, with the bard, the disappearance of the oral tradition as a living form of art. The technique of balladising within the traditional formulae, remarkably, did remain extant in some remote oases of illiteracy (mostly among Islamicized Bosnians) right into the twentieth century. In the 1930's the scholars Milman Parry and Albert B. Lord, realising that it might serve as an analogue to the epic milieu from which the Homeric poems emerged, made intensive studies in this field and their work contributed significantly to the solution of the 'Homeric question'. However, the oral tradition was no longer at the heart of things and if for that reason alone its product, whilst being the subject of considerable academic interest, could not amount to much more than pastiche. The 'classic' epic ballads from which this selection is taken, on the other hand, remain at the very centre of Serbian culture as justifiable objects of pride.

As well as recording the national ballads, Karadžić published many philological works, including the first authoritative Serbian Dictionary and a Grammar, basing both upon a particularly pure and expressive form of the language as spoken in parts of Hercegovina. In doing so, and at the same time, he instituted a major reform of the orthography of the language, both by rationalising and simplifying the Cyrillic alphabet, and by supporting the official adoption of a parallel Latin orthography with some diacritic signs (the '*latinica*') based on the same principles (namely that spelling should reflect pronunciation, and that each letter should represent one sound, and vice versa).

Karadžić was not undiscriminating in his work of collection. He was well aware that the quality and ability of the bards of his day varied considerably, as they will have done throughout history. Himself steeped in the traditional ballads from boyhood, he deliberately sought out bards of the highest reputation, and generally only included in his published collections those versions of ballads which were of the highest artistic standard. He tells how, having heard an indifferent performance of one potentially fine ballad, he had to wait twenty years before being able to find and record a much superior version from a better bard.

In Karadžić's time there were three outstanding male bards, **Filip Višnjić** (pronounced 'Vishnyich'), **Tešan Podrugović** ('Teshan Podrugovich'), and **Starac Milija** ('Starats Miliya'), and two exceptional women, **Živana** ('Zhivana') and **Jeca** ('Yetsa'), both blind. The men were far from being pale aesthetes, singing of heroism in the abstract.

Višnjić, blind from the age of eight, had at the age of twenty escaped the torture and slaughter of his family by the Turks. (He could not see, but he could hear his uncle singing defiantly as he was led to execution). He took part in the First Serbian Uprising, earning renown for maintaining the morale of the Serbian forces during the siege of Loznica by his ballad-singing. Thereafter he travelled widely as a professional bard, performing in villages, towns, and in Turkish courts (for which he slily kept a special repertoire), and became rich and famous until his death in 1834. It is reliably reported that his artistry was such that he could regularly reduce an audience to tears when performing the more tragic ballads.

Podrugović was a huge man who, at the age of twenty-five drove off a group of Turks who were trying to rape his sister, killing one of them. As a result he had to take to the woods as an outlaw, and did well in that trade. He fought as a soldier in the First Serbian Uprising, distinguishing himself in battle, but deserted "to avoid the necessity of killing his captain, who had offended him". He was making a poor living cutting and selling reeds when Karadžić found him in 1814, and took down over twenty ballads at his dictation. In 1815 he fought in the Second Uprising, but again absented himself from the army and went to Bosnia, where he had the misfortune to kill a Turkish Bey and was obliged once more to become an outlaw. Whilst attempting to rejoin the Serbian army he was fatally wounded quarrelling with some Turks in an inn. His speciality as a bard was that he spoke his ballads instead of singing them. Karadžić considered him to be the greatest of all the bards of his time.

Starac Milija, a farmer, was in his fifties before being obliged to abandon his land and flee after being involved in a fight with some Turks. It was with great reluctance that he obeyed an order of the then Serbian ruler, Miloš Obrenović, to come and sing for Karadžić in 1822, when he was an old man so weak from wounds and decrepitude that he was unable (or at any rate unwilling) to perform without constant and plentiful doses of brandy. After declaiming four ballads he decided that the whole business of writing them down was a stupid waste of time and returned in a huff to his farm, where he died the following year. Nevertheless, one of the ballads which he recited during this brief meeting was 'Banovich Strahinya' – one of the longest and arguably the finest of all the recorded Serbian epic ballads. Of the blind women bards much less is known. As might be expected, they travelled less, and they generally attached themselves to monasteries.

Živana and **Jeca** both sang at Zemun, just across the Sava from Belgrade. Blind Jeca it was who gave Karadžić 'The Death of Voivoda Priyezda' – one of the best-known and possibly one of the most perfect of the shorter ballads in content, style, and balance.

All of them stamped their individual artistic personalities upon their balladising, even though each was operating within the strict conventions of the craft. Višnjić is remarkable for the purity and classical perfection of his style, and he excelled in the most serious and noble ballads. Podrugović is somewhat more fluent and innovative, more ready to extend the boundaries of prosody and language, and reveals an irrepressible sense of humour in appropriate contexts. Starac Milija is something of a combination of both, with an amazing grasp of structure and balance in long stories.

The bards obviously had to have prodigious memories. Karadžić noted that Podrugović knew over a hundred ballads in addition to those in the published collections, and that if he heard a new ballad he would retain it after one hearing (and usually produce an improved version soon afterwards). The average length of the ballads is about 200 lines. Podrugović must therefore have had at least 20,000 lines of formulaic verse in his memory, and he was not a professional bard. The superior strength of memory in illiterate people is, of course, a recognized and well-documented fact, but it remains surprising to all of us who rely upon written records as a substitute for it.

The Epic in the Making, by S. Koljević (Oxford, 1980) provides an excellent account of the historical background, and of the nature and methods of the bards themselves. It also includes useful commentaries on most of the ballads in this collection, and an extensive bibliography. *The Life and Times of Vuk Stefanović Karadžić,* by Duncan Wilson (Ann Arbor, 1986) is a comprehensive survey of the philologist's work and his place in history. *The Making of Homeric Verse* by Milman Parry (Oxford, 1971) and *The Singer of Tales* by Albert B. Lord (Cambridge, Mass., 1960) are academic works relevant to the 'Homeric question'.

3
THE SERBIAN LANGUAGE AND THE PROSODY OF THE BALLADS

Jakob Grimm, generally acknowledged to be one of the greatest experts of his own or any other age in the field of comparative literature, on reviewing Vuk Karadžić's first published selection of Serbian songs in 1815 commented: "Of all Slavonic races, the Serbs are by virtue of their language (so rich and so suitable for poetry) the most blessed with poems, songs and stories, and it looks as if the good God had by this rich gift of popular poetry wished to make up to them for their lack of books."

In general terms, Serbian is a language in which little or no stress is placed upon any syllable in a word: in this regard it is more analogous to French than to English or Russian. The main rule is that such stress as there is never comes on the last syllable. In the best spoken Serbian each syllable is pronounced evenly and clearly, in contrast to the speech-pattern of a stressed language such as English, where the heavy emphasis on certain syllables leads to 'subordinate' syllables being hurried over or almost lost. It follows that the rhythms and cadences in Serbian speech arise from the varying tones and length of syllables, rather than from the percussive rhythms generated by a succession of stressed and unstressed syllables, as in English.

Thanks to Vuk Karadžić's reforms, the orthography of Serbian is straightforward. It is completely phonetic: every letter is pronounced exactly as it is written, and there are no irregularities or exceptions (again, unlike Russian). In speech the vowels vary in length and pitch, so varying the length of syllables and, of course, the surrounding consonants also have their effect on 'length' in the prosodic sense. Nevertheless, it is quite possible for a non-Serbian speaker, having learned the significance of the (few) modified consonants, to read and even read aloud passages of Serbian quite adequately, even without understanding the meaning, and to pronounce the names of people and places correctly.

INTRODUCTION

A central feature of the main South Slavonic language (which, largely for political convenience, came to be called Serbo-Croat) is the adoption in writing of the German *j* (always pronounced as consonantal *y*). This letter, when followed by *-e*, reveals the fundamental difference between the three principal dialects of what is, in its grammar, its syntax, and the great bulk of its vocabulary, the same language. These dialects are regional, rather than racial or "national" and there is considerable overlapping. The difference between them is simply illustrated by the name of the Adriatic port, Rijeka. The word simply means 'river' and, indeed, the town was called 'Fiume' when it was under Italian rule. In the eastern region (generally in Serbia proper), 'river' is *reka*, in the western (typically in Croatia, Bosnia, and Hercegovina) it is *rijeka* (pronounced 'riyeka'), and in parts of Dalmatia and its hinterland it is spelled and pronounced *rika*. This stems from the way people in the various regions came to differ, over time, in their pronunciation of words containing the Old Slavonic letter Ѣ (yat). Since it is the most obvious and easily identifiable difference between them, the principal dialects are classified as the **'e'** dialect *(ekavski)*, the **'je'** (or **'ije'**) dialect *(jekavski)*, and the **'i'** dialect *(ikavski)*. Serbian ballads appear in all these various dialects, reflecting the widespread origins of the bards and, indeed, the extent of the Serbian diaspora.

Native speakers of the language know both the (modified) Cyrillic and Latin alphabets. The Serbs, Montenegrins, and Macedonians generally prefer to use the Cyrillic which they regard as their patrimony, while the Croats, Dalmatians, and Bosnians always use the Latin alphabet (as do the Slovenes, whose language is otherwise markedly different). I have throughout this Introduction and the Notes used the modified Latin alphabet, rather than the Cyrillic, in order to make everything more accessible to English-speaking people. In the translations, however, I have adopted a simple form of transliteration, because the ballads are intended to be read cursively, as verse, and even though the modified Latin alphabet is inherently simple, it is still foreign to English eyes and demands a perceptible 'change of gear' to read when it is mixed in with English. (It requires an effort, for instance, to recognize *Car* as Tsar, and to remember that *Jelica* does not alliterate with Angelica!). I have set out my system of transliteration on page xxxvii . This also includes a full explanation of the modified Latin alphabet.

The metrical scheme of the originals is the *deseterac* (pron. 'deseterats'), a line of ten syllables with a slight pause, or caesura, after the fourth. No word may 'cross' the caesura. In earlier times much verse, both epic and lyrical, was set in a line of from fourteen to sixteen syllables – the *bugarštica* (pron. 'bugarshtitsa') – but this form appears eventually to have been rejected by the bards as too facile for epic verse. It will be appreciated that the combination of the fixed caesura and the unstressed last-syllable rule means that the deseterac consists of two unequal 'halves', the first having four syllables and the second six, and that the last syllable of each 'half' must be unaccented.

Serbian is a highly inflected language with three genders, seven cases in singular and plural, fully declined pronouns and adjectives (the latter having both definite and indefinite forms), and two aspects of the verb, each fully conjugated. The inflected nature of the language allowed the bard some flexibility in word-order, but less than that available to the ancient Latin and Greek poets who were working within similarly inflected languages, since Serbian imposes severe restrictions on the placing many parts of the verb 'to be' (whether used alone or as the auxiliary verb) and of many pronouns. Of course, the need to inflect words in itself presented the bard with many intractable problems in fitting words into the severely restricted format of the *deseterac*. The Serbian bards would solve these difficulties by a variety of devices such as juggling the order of words, inserting 'unnecessary' epithets or linking-words, inverting names or using alternative forms of them, elision of syllables and, *in extremis*, using inconsistent dialect or simply fudging the grammar. A device very frequently used was to address a personality in the vocative case as though he or she were present (for, as well as having dramatic effect, this would often produce a convenient extra syllable!). I have by no means always translated such things literally, and have generally kept names of people and places in the nominative case throughout.

4
NOTES ON TRANSLATION

The translation of verse from one language to another raises vexed questions of metre, and these are particularly acute when one language is quantitative, like Serbian, and the other is stressed, like English. In the past, poets as distinguished as Spenser and Tennyson have attempted to reproduce in English verse the quantitative measures of the Latin and Greek classics, with negligible success. The stressed syllable in an English word is so crucial that to move the stress within it can render the word incomprehensible, or can even change its entire meaning, and the brutal fact is that the stress does not necessarily fall on the 'long' vowel. It follows that the classical measures of iamb and trochee have a quite different meaning in quantitative verse from that ascribed to them in accentual-syllabic verse. Serbian verse being quantitative, the Serbian *deseterac* does not sound or 'feel' like an English trochaic pentameter, even though it may look like one on paper. I have therefore made no attempt to set these ballads in a metrical line which purports to approximate to that of the originals. Instead, I have sought to transcribe the traditional Serbian form of verse into its nearest counterpart – the pentameter of traditional English blank verse, basically though not invariably iambic. I have in consequence not felt bound to reproduce the caesura. I have, however, deliberately accepted the discipline of the strict decasyllabic line, in homage to those countless Serbian bards who down the ages struggled to cast their abounding poetic inspiration in the stern mould of the *deseterac*.

As to the content of the ballads, I have throughout sought to transcribe both the sense and the musicality of the words, according to their context. There are some passages where it is possible to translate literally, but in most cases to do so would result in doggerel, and would give the English reader a quite false impression of the effect that the Serbian bard was seeking to make: I have always tried to convey this latter. There are, of course, many standard expressions: swords are always 'bright' and servants are always 'faithful', throats are always 'white' and wine is always 'cool' or 'red'. I strongly suspect that most of these formulae derive as much from prosodic convenience as from poetic necessity, and it is noticeable that the most effective bards used them the least. I have usually translated them literally, but in the case of some, such as the 'warlike lance', I have not always repeated the epithet in the middle of a fast-moving description of battle, for instance.

In connection with obsolete things generally, especially weapons, I have looked for equivalent terms. For example, before firearms appeared Serbian heroes were much given to assaulting their foes with a *perni buzdovan*. This translates literally as a 'feathered mace', which makes a pretty fairy-like impression in English: I have translated it as 'spiked bludgeon' because that is what it really was! As to weights and measures, my approach has been as varied as the bards' was insouciant. The standard measure of weight, frequently mentioned, was the *oka*, or oke, of about 2½ pounds. In many cases I have simply called it an 'oke', even though it means that one hero's bludgeon weighed a hundredweight and a half! On the other hand, where the same hero is portrayed drinking wine from a 'jug of twelve okes' (33 pounds), I have rendered it 'of five-gallon size' to convey the impression of size with no more pretence at accuracy than that intended by the bard. The Serbs were not interested in accountancy. A 'great deal of money' was what was meant by *tovar blaga* – literally 'a load of treasure'. The size of the load was never mentioned: it could have been a pouch, a sack, a pack-horse pannier, or a cartload! I have translated it as the context suggests. A 'very large number' (of soldiers, wedding-guests, sheep, etc.) is almost always 'twelve thousand'. The bards would probably have reckoned that 'ten thousand' has a good ring, and sounds a lot, but, unfortunately, that number has only five syllables in Serbian, while *dvanaest hiljada*, with six, fits neatly into the second 'half' of the *deseterac*!

The titles of rulers and noblemen can be a source of confusion. Basically, among the Serbs an Emperor was a Tsar *(car)*, a King was a Kral *(kralj)*, and a Prince or Chieftain was a Knez. Among the Turks, the supreme ruler was the Sultan, and subordinate rulers were a Pasha *(paša)*, a Bey *(beg)*, and an Aga. The matter became complicated after the Turkish conquest, when Turkish grandees came to be referred to in the ballads by Slavonic titles. For the sake of simplicity, I have throughout these translations kept Serbian titles for Serbian rulers, and have called all foreign rulers Kings except for the 'Turkish Tsar', whom I have called the Sultan. Pashas, Beys and Agas, of course, are called by those titles when they so appear in the original. Where necessary, I have made individual notes in the Appendix.

My selection of ballads for this collection has been based on two factors: firstly, that they should cover a reasonably wide variety of historical range, style, and content, and secondly, that they should have the quality of classics, namely that one continues to enjoy them even after many years (and even after the labour of transcribing them into English verse!) For what, after all, are 'classics' in any form of art other than those works which continue to hold the attention and exercize the imagination even after frequent repetition? In the case of the Serbian Epic Ballads the analogy with music is close: the development of a formalised style and rigid rules of harmony and counterpoint enabled literally hundreds of composers to turn out adequate sonatas, symphonies, choral works, and operas in the Western Europe of the turn of the eighteenth and nineteenth centuries, just as a rigid convention enabled many jobbing bards to turn out acceptable ballads in Serbian, but just as Haydn and Mozart, working within the conventional style, could produce works that are still at the forefront of the repertoire after two hundred years whilst the vast majority of their contemporaries are but 'Interesting Historical Figures', so the greatest of the Serbian bards were able to transcend the limitations of their art to produce works which can properly claim to be classics of European epic literature in their own right.

There follow on the next pages a full explanation of the modified Latin orthography, its pronunciation, and the system of transliteration which I have used in the translations and in the notes to them, together with a comparative table of the Cyrillic, Latin, and English alphabets.

The numbers in the text refer to the Appendix, which contains short notes about each of the ballads and about some of the personalities and places named in them. The notes also contain explanations of certain words and expressions which have been left in the (transliterated) original. Where possible, they also give the name of the bard whose version of the ballad was recorded in the original collections.

There are a number of 'standard' openings for the ballads. These three- or four-line flourishes do not necessarily have any direct connection with the ballad that they introduce, but were often intended to do no more than settle the listeners and, perhaps, put them in the mood to hear more. Wishing that it may serve those same ends, I venture to end my Introduction to this anthology of the Serbian Epic Ballads with one such opening, which I respectfully hope may be appropriate:

Braćo mila i družino draga!
Ja ne pjevam što je meni drago,
Već ja pjevam da vas razveselim ...

Dear brothers all, and good companions!
I do not sing for my delight alone,
I sing for you, to gladden all your hearts ...

G.N.W.L.
Poole, Dorset.
June 2001

NOTES ON TRANSLITERATION AND PRONOUNCIATION

1. VOWELS

The five vowels are pronounced plainly and flatly, much as in Italian, wherever they come in a word (including at the end of it). There are no irregularities or exceptions:

- **a**   as in   **last**
- **e**   as in   **let**
- **i**   as in   **leek**
- **o**   as in   **lawn**
- **u**   as in   **loot**

NOTE: The letter **r** is rolled so strongly that it can virtually act as a vowel. When this occurs I have made it **er**. (e.g. *Vučitrn* = Vuchitern).

2. CONSONANTS

The pronunciation of certain consonants is modified by diacritic signs (they appear only on consonants). I have transliterated them as follows:

c	becomes	**ts** as in **bats**
č and **ć**	become	**ch** as in **church**. (The Serbian letters do not sound exactly the same, but the difference is minimal)
đ(dj), and **dž** become		**dj** as in **judge** (These do sound different: the *dž* is heavier)
š	becomes	**sh** as in **shoe**
ž	becomes	**zh** as in **pleasure**

And note:

- **g** always hard, as in **golf**
- **h** heavily aspirated, as in Scottish **loch**
- **s** always plain **s**, as in lo<u>s</u>t (never pronounced **sh**, as in German <u>**S**</u>tuben, or **z**, as in English hou<u>s</u>e**).**

The letter *j* is always pronounced as consonantal *y*, as in German. When it comes between two vowels (*-ija, -ije*, etc) I have made it **y**, unless the word already has an obvious English form (e.g. *Srbija* = Serbia). In diphthongs (*-aj,- oj* , etc) I have made it **i** (e.g. *Vojvoda* = Voivoda).

3. "SOFT" CONSONANTS

Some words contain, or even end in, *lj* or *nj*. The *nj* is as Spanish *ñ*, and the *lj* is similarly "softened". At the end of a word, or before a consonant, they defy transliteration: I have simply left off the *-j* and made a note in the Appendix (e.g. *Kralj* = Kral, and *Banjska* = Banska).

The three alphabets, Cyrillic, Latin, and English, are set out opposite.

THE ALPHABETS

CYRILLIC	LATIN	ENGLISH
А а	A a	a
Б б	B b	b
В в	V v	v
Г г	G g	g
Д д	D d	d
Ђ ђ	Đ đ	dj (see note 2)
Е е	E e	e
Ж ж	Ž ž	zh
З з	Z z	z
И и	I i	i
Ј ј	J j	y (see note 2)
К к	K k	k
Л л	L l	l
Љ љ	Lj lj	l (see note 3)
М м	M m	m
Н н	N n	n
Њ њ	Nj nj	n (see note 3)
О о	O o	o
П п	P p	p
Р р	R r	r
С с	S s	s
Т т	T t	t
Ћ ћ	Ć ć	ch (see note 2)
У у	U u	u
Ф ф	F f	f
Х х	H h	h
Ц ц	C c	ts
Ч ч	Č č	ch (see note 2)
Џ џ	Dž dž	dj (see note 2)
Ш ш	Š š	sh

BALLADS OF
THE MEDIAEVAL EMPIRE

1
Tsar Dushan's Wedding

When Stefan, Tsar of all the Serbs,[1] would wed,
The maiden that he sought lived far away
In Ledjan, in the distant Latin lands,[2]
Where reigned Mihailo, a great Latin King;[3]
The maiden was his daughter, Roksanda.[4]
The Tsar proposed: the King gave his consent.

It was by written letters that the Tsar
Had courted Roksanda, his bride-to-be.
But now he called his Vezir,[5] and he said:
"My trusty servant Todor, my Vezir,
To Ledjan go, as my ambassador!
There, parley with the father of my bride,
Good King Mihailo. All arrangements make
As to my wedding-day. When shall we come
To fetch the bride? How many guests may bring?
And when you see the maiden, Roksanda,
You must decide if she is fit to be
My Tsaritsa, and Mistress of this Realm.
If such she seem to you, we are betrothed,
And on her finger you shall put this ring."

Todor replied: "My lord, my Tsar, I will!"
And then he journeyed to the Latin lands
Until, at last, he came to Ledjan town,
Where Mihailo the King received him well.
For seven days they feasted and drank wine,
But then Todor the Vezir said: "My friend,
King Mihailo! The Tsar has not sent me
To spend my days in Ledjan drinking wine,
But rather that we both may be agreed
On all that touches on the wedding-day.

When should my lord, the Tsar, come for his bride?
How many guests may bring? He also wished
That I should see Roksanda with my eyes,
And signify betrothal with a ring."

Then answered King Mihailo: "My good friend
Todor, no need for all this questioning!
The Tsar may come whenever he may please;
As many guests may bring as he may wish.
But one request: the Tsar should not invite
That pair of nephews called Voyinovich[6] –
Vukashin, and his brother Petrashin –
For both are drunkards, always quarrelling;
They're sure to drink too much and start a fight.
'Twould be embarrassing for you and us,
For here in Ledjan City we have laws
Which make the penalty for brawling hard.
I promise, you shall see Roksanda soon,
And give the ring, according to the law."

But when the night was at its darkest hour
They brought the maiden to him : nor was there
A waxen candle lit, to see her by.
But wise Todor was in no way dismayed:
He took the Tsar's own ring, of shining gold,
Inset with pearls and glowing precious stones,
And saw her, by the light it gave, to seem
More beautiful than flesh and blood can be.
He put the Tsar's betrothal ring upon
Roksanda's finger, and he gave to her
A thousand golden ducats, as a gift.
And then her brothers led her from the room.

And when the light of dawn brought forth the day
Todor the Tsar's Vezir prepared himself,
And set off on his way to fair Prizren.[7]

And when at last he came to Prizren town

Tsar Stefan summoned him, and questioned him:
"Todor, my faithful servant, my Vezir!
Did you behold the maiden, Roksanda?
And did you give her my betrothal ring?
What said the King?" And Todor made reply:
"My Tsar! I saw the maiden, and have put
Your ring upon her finger. She is such
That in all Serbia there's none to match!
The King, Mihailo, fairly spoke with me:
'As to the maiden, fetch her when you will.
Bring guests, as many as you may desire.'
But he requests that you do not invite
Your nephews called Voyinovich – those two –
For both are drunkards, always quarrelling;
They're sure to drink too much and start a fight.
'Twould be embarrassing for you and him,
For there in Ledjan City they have laws
Which make the penalty for brawling hard."

And when the Serbian Tsar Stefan heard this
He struck his hand upon his knee, and cried:
"Almighty God, preserve me from my wrath!
That precious pair – brothers Voyinovich!
Has their ill-fame, then, spread abroad so far
That they can soil my reputation thus?
As soon as all the celebrating's done
I'll hang them both upon the city gates
Of Vuchitern,[8] for shaming me like this!"

The Tsar assembled then his wedding-guests.
Twelve thousand was their number, and they all
Set out across the plain of Kosovo.[9]

As they approached the walls of Vuchitern
The two young brothers called Voyinovich
Watched them go past, and wondered to themselves:
"What has so vexed our uncle? Why is it

That he has not invited us as guests?
Someone has foully slandered us to him –
And may the living flesh drop off his bones!
The Tsar is travelling to far-off lands
With no stout hero in his train – no one
Of his own kin to stand by if, amongst
The foreigners some treachery befall.
'Tis known of old, Latins are perfidious:
No good towards our uncle do they wish,
But, uninvited thus, we dare not go."

    Then out spoke their old mother: "My two sons!
Remember now your brother in the hills,
Milosh the shepherd,[10] tending there his flocks –
The youngest but the bravest of you all;
And more than that, Tsar Dushan knows him not.
Send him a message. Bid him come at once
To Vuchitern, but do not tell him of
The thing that now concerns us. No, tell him
That I am close to death, and must see him
To bless him, that no curse may be on him.
Tell him to come at once, with no delay.
Bid him: 'Make haste, our mother's time is near.'"

    And what their mother said, the brothers did.
In haste they wrote a letter to Milosh
The shepherd boy, their brother, sending it
To where he dwelt upon the hills of Shar,[11]
And thus it read: "Milosh, our brother born!
Come home to Vuchitern – do not delay!
Our own dear aged mother's close to death:
You must receive her blessing while she lives
So that no curse may linger on your head."

    The letter came to Milosh in the hills,
And when he read it tears flowed down his cheeks.
His thirty shepherd comrades were amazed:

"O Milosh, chief amongst us!" they cried out,
"Writings have come before, which have not caused
Your tears to flow. What says this writing now?
We pray you, tell us, for the love of God!"

Milosh stood up, and so addressed the men:
"My friends, O my dear brothers, shepherds all!
This letter's from my home, my very hearth:
It says my aged mother's near to death.
She calls me home, to bless me while she lives,
So that no curse may linger on my head.
Now you must tend my sheep upon these hills
While I depart, and till I shall return."
And Milosh then went home to Vuchitern.

As he approached his home, that noble hall,
His brothers came to meet him on the road,
And after them his aged mother came.
And, seeing her, Milosh the Shepherd cried:
"My brothers dear, in God's name, what is this?
Why do you tell of sorrow where none is?"
"Sorrow there is indeed!" his brothers said.

Milosh embraced his brothers, kissed their cheeks,
And, going to his mother, kissed her hand.
And when they had embraced they told the tale
Of all that had befallen: how the Tsar
Had gone away to claim his chosen bride
Among the Latins, in those far-off lands,
But had not taken them with him as guests.
"But you, Milosh, our brother born, must go.
Our uncle knows you not. Go after them
And follow the assembly from afar.
If treachery befall, you will be there
To save our uncle and, if all be well,
Unknown you can return, with no harm done."

Then Milosh, hesitating not at all,

Said: "Brothers dear, God help me, and I will!
Who should I serve, if not my noble kin?"

    The brothers started to prepare him then.
The horse was Petrashin's care: Vukashin
Equipped Milosh himself. First a fine smock –
Below the waist of pure cloth of gold,
Above the waist it was of white silk made.
Above the smock three jerkins fine he wore;
A dolman then, with thirty silver clasps,
And over that a tunic of gold mail
All made of massive plates – ten pounds each weighed;
Upon his legs gold greaves, and pantaloons;
And over all, a heavy shepherd's coat;
Upon his head a shepherd's black fur hat.
So did he seem a black Bulgarian[12]
Whom e'en his brothers could not recognize.

    They handed him a heavy warrior's lance;
He took the shining sword his father'd borne.
Petrashin brought the great dun horse, Kulash,
Its heavy coat and mane all clipped and trimmed
So that the Tsar, their uncle, might not know't.

    Then, carefully, they counselled Milosh so:
"Now Milosh, when you reach the wedding guests
They'll ask you who you are, and whence you've come.
Tell them you've left the land of Karavlah,[13]
Tell them: 'I served the Turk, Beg Radul-beg:
That skinflint wouldn't pay me for my work,
So I cleared off, into the wider world
To find a better master I can serve.
I heard the Tsar was travelling to claim
His bride, and taking many wedding-guests,
So I have come to follow in his train.
I hope, maybe, to earn myself a crust
And, maybe, good red wine, by serving you.'
And, Milosh, mark this well – restrain your horse!

Hold fast the reins! He is of noble stock,
And used to going with the Tsar's own steeds."

Then Milosh turned his horse and spurred away,
And followed in the wedding-party's tracks.

He reached them as they came to Zagoryé.
The gorgeously-apparelled wedding-guests
Saw him, and asked : "Whence come you, young Bulgar?"
And, from a distance, Milosh told the tale
His brothers earlier had made him learn.
At this, they took him in most willingly:
"Welcome amongst us, young Bulgarian!
Another one shall make good company."

While they were journeying upon the road
Young Milosh slept, for, on the hills of Shar,
His habit was to sleep among the sheep
All afternoon. So slept he as he rode.
The reins went loose, the horse raised up its head,
And blundered through the guests, until it came
Up to the very horse upon whose back
The Tsar was riding, and took station there.

The courtiers rushed up to beat him off,
But Tsar Stefan forbade them: "Do not beat
This young Bulgar, for shepherds learn to sleep
This way, upon the mountains with their sheep.
Do not chastise him – wake him up, instead."

The courtiers and noblemen obeyed:
"Come on, wake up, you young Bulgarian!
May God preserve your mother, who has borne
A son like you, and given us a king
To take his place among the wedding-guests!"

Milosh Voyinovich awoke from sleep.
He found his horse was walking by the Tsar's,
And saw the Tsar's dark eyes regarding him.
He seized the reins and rode off to one side

And there, with copper goad, he whipped his horse.
So furiously it leaped up in the air –
As high as three long lances stood on end –
And then as high as four – then higher yet:
Up to the sky – no man could say how high!
Live fire poured from its mouth, and from its nose
Blue flames! The guests, twelve thousand, stood and watched
The horse and the Bulgarian shepherd-boy.
They saw the horse's mettle, and, amazed,
They said amongst themselves: "Dear God, how strange!
That horse is wonderful – the rider's not!
A horse as fine as that is seldom seen.
The Tsar's own sister's family had one
Like that – the family Voyinovich!"

There were three scoundrels in the crowd that watched:
Vuk Djakovitsa was the name of one,
The second was Yanko Nestopolyats,
The third young man was called Priyepolyats.
These three conspired: "That shepherd's horse is good!
There is not one so good among the guests' –
The Tsar himself does not possess its like.
Let's find a place to catch him on his own:
With any luck, he'll be an easy touch!"

So, when they reached a rocky cleft beside
The road, these scoundrels lay in waiting there,
And when Milosh came by they said to him:
"Now, come along, our young Bulgarian friend!
There is no robbery in fair exchange!
Now, you just let us have that horse of yours,
And we'll give you a better one by far,
And you shall have a hundred ducats, too:
On top of that some oxen, and a plough
To till the earth, and so to grow your corn."
But Milosh said: "Leave me alone, you rogues!

I want no better horse than this – besides,
I've barely learned to pacify this one.
A hundred ducats – what's the use of that?
I don't know how to weigh them in a scales
And, as for counting them – I cannot count!
What use are oxen and a plough to me?
My father had no plough, but even so
He brought me up, and got my bread for me."

But then those ruffians menaced him, and said:
"Enough of this, you young Bulgarian fool!
If you'll not give that horse in fair exchange
We'll force you to, no matter what you do!"

Then Milosh said: "You may take towns by force,
And lands: there are enough of you, I fear.
So I'll exchange this horse, for otherwise
I'd have to walk, and it's too far for that."

He stopped the horse and put his hand inside
His coat to take (the others thought) his goad.
But it was not his goad that he drew out –
It was his bludgeon, six-spiked, gold-adorned!
With it Milosh struck Vuk Djakovitsa:
Lightly he struck, but Vuk spun round three times.
Milosh Voyinovich called out to him:
"Three times you've spun, my lad, just as you have
Three vines in Djakovitsa, where you live!"

Then Yanko Nestpolyats turned and fled,
But Milosh spurred his horse and caught him up.
He swung his bludgeon and he struck his back,
And four times did he turn head-over-heels.
"Bear up, my little Yanko!" Milosh cried,
"Four times you've cartwheeled here: four apple trees
You have in Nestopolye, where you live!"

Priyepolyats fled from him, full of fear,
But Milosh spurred his horse and caught him up,
And with his bludgeon he so battered him

DUSHAN'S WEDDING

That seven times he somersaulted there.
"Hold up, young Priyepolyats!" Milosh cried,
"When you get home to Priyepolye, think
How you can thrill the women, telling them
Of how you stole the black Bulgarian's horse!"
    And, turning, Milosh rode to join the throng.

    At last they came to Ledjan, that fair town,
And round about in fields they pitched their tents.
They brought out oats to feed the Tsar's own steeds,
But for Milosh's horse there were none left.
So Milosh took a bucket, and went round
And took a handful here and there until
He'd filled the bucket: thus he fed his horse.

    And after that he went into an inn.
"Landlord, bring wine for me to drink!" he said.
    The publican would not. Instead, he cried:
"Get out of here, you black Bulgarian!
You should have brought your wooden drinking-trough
If you want wine to drink, for I'll not set
My golden cups before the likes of you!"

    Milosh regarded him a little while,
Then struck him with his fist upon the mouth.
He did not strike him hard, but yet he broke
Three teeth, and knocked them down the landlord's throat.

    The publican then changed his tune, and begged:
"Enough, good Sir! Don't hit me any more!
Straightway I'll serve you all the wine you want,
E'en if the Tsar himself must go without!"

    But Milosh, wearying of talk, could wait
No longer, and himself poured out his wine.

    And so, while Milosh thus refreshed himself,
The sun rose, and the day dawned bright and clear.
And then from Ledjan's walls a voice rang out:
"Oyez! O hear ye, Serbian Tsar Stefan!

Behold! Upon the plain beneath the town
The champion of King Mihailo waits!
He challenges the bravest of your knights
To meet in single combat with him there.
And if you fail this challenge, then be sure
Nor you, nor all your guests shall leave this place,
Far less shall take Roksanda as your bride!"

And when the Serbian Tsar Stefan heard this
He sent a shining herald forth to go
Among the wedding-guests and call aloud:
"Is there amongst you not a hero born,
Equipped and armed, and ready for the fray,
Who in the Lists of Honour now will fight
For his Tsar's sake? He'll have a fine reward!"

But in that throng there was not one who dared.
The Tsar then beat his hand upon his knee
And bitterly he cried: "Now help me God!
If I but had my nephews here with me –
That pair of brothers called Voyinovich –
They would have gone to battle for me now."

And as he thus made wail Milosh approached,
And led his horse up to the very tent
Before which sat the Serbian Tsar Stefan.
"My lord, my Tsar!" said he, "May I go forth
And fight this fellow for you in the Lists?"

And Stefan, Tsar of all the Serbs, replied:
"You may, you may, my young Bulgarian friend!
It is not fitting, but, if you should win
You shall receive a fine reward from me."
Then Milosh mounted on his fiery horse.
He turned away from where the Tsar was sat
And couched his lance – but held it back-to-front!

The Serbian Tsar Stefan called out to him:
"My son, you've got your lance the wrong way round!
You must reverse it, point towards the front –

DUSHAN'S WEDDING

The Latins otherwise will laugh at you!"

Milosh Voyinovich called back: "My Tsar!
Let Tsardom be your care, and leave me mine!
If any difficulty should befall
I'll quickly turn it round the other way.
But otherwise, if all goes well, why then
It suits me just exactly as it is."

And with those words he rode off to the field
Of battle, on the plain 'neath Ledjan's walls.

The Latin maidens, watching from the town,
Saw Milosh coming, and they laughed aloud:
"Dear God! What sort of challenger is this?
A ragged boy – no shirt upon his back!
Rejoice, O Royal Champion – take your ease!
There is no need for you to draw your sword,
Nor yet bestir yourself to bloody it!"

Then Milosh rode up to the tent where sat
The Latin champion, whose bay horse stood
Beside him, tethered to his upturned lance.
And when he came before him Milosh cried:
"Now then, pale Latin, stand up! – On your feet!
I challenge you in battle to the death!"

The pale-skinned Latin champion did not move:
"Get out of here, you black Bulgarian!
I'll not begrime my sword with your low blood,
Nor beat your back, that has no shirt on it!"

Milosh raged: "Get up, you Latin lily!
And as for those fine clothes that you've got on –
I'll wear them, after I have dealt with you!"

At that the Latin jumped up to his feet
And, mounting on his fiery battle-horse,
He charged across the field to where Milosh
Stood waiting, like a target in the butts.
The furious Latin champion hurled his lance
With deadly aim to pierce Milosh's breast.

But Milosh had his bludgeon in his hand.
He swung the bludgeon: struck the Latin's lance –
And smashed it in three pieces as it flew!

The pale-skinned Latin champion shouted: "Wait!
Hold hard, you black Bulgarian! That lance
Was not a proper one – 'tis treachery!
You wait for me – I'll fetch another lance."
With that, he rode away across the field.

Milosh Voyinovich called after him:
"Not so! You wait, pale Latin! Though you wish
To flee from me, yet shall you not escape!"
He spurred his horse and chased him as he fled
Up to the very gates of Ledjan town.
But now the gates of Ledjan town were shut.
Then Milosh cast his lance, and spitted him
Like any fowl, upon the city gates.

He then cut off the blond-haired Latin's head
And thrust it in the nosebag of his horse.
He took the Latin champion's bay horse
And, leading it, he went back to the Tsar.
"My Tsar! I bring the fellow's head," he cried.

The Tsar rewarded him with untold wealth:
"My son!" he said, "Take this, and get you wine,
And you shall be most honoured, in my name!"

No sooner had Milosh sat down to drink,
Than from the Latin town a voice rang out:
"Behold, O Tsar! Beneath these city walls
There stand three battle-horses on the field.
Those horses are all saddled and equipped.
Upon their backs are fixed three shining swords,
Their naked blades are pointing to the sky;
And you must now leap over all of them!
And if you fail this test, then nevermore
Shall you leave here, nor take your bride away!"

DUSHAN'S WEDDING

Once more the herald called among the guests:
"Is there no mother's son with hero's heart
Amongst you all, who's ready, for his Tsar,
To overleap those battle-horses three,
Upon whose backs are stood three shining swords?"

But such a hero was not to be found.

The young 'Bulgarian' then stood up, and went
Before the tent where sat the Serbian Tsar
And boldly said: "My lord, my noble Tsar!
Those horses there – may I jump over them?"

"You may, my darling son!" the Tsar replied,
"But first, I pray you, shed that overcoat –
The Devil take the tailor who made that!"

Milosh did not obey; instead, he said:
"My noble Tsar, you sit and drink good wine,
And do not care about my overcoat!
It will not hinder me, for under it
There beats a hero's heart. I will not fail.
For if a sheep is troubled by its coat
The sheep's no good and neither is the fleece."

Then Milosh walked on to the level plain,
Leading his great dun horse, until he came
To where the three great battle-horses stood.
He stopped his horse, and whispered in its ear:
"Stay here and wait for me: I'll mount you soon."

Then, going to the other side, he turned
And raced across the field: he bounded up
High over those three horses, and the swords
That bristled on their backs, and landed, safe,
In his own horse's saddle! Then he rode,
Leading the other horses, to the Tsar.

A little time then passed, before again
A voice was heard to cry from Ledjan's walls:
"Now hearken! You, the Tsar of all the Serbs!

Come here, beneath this shining tower, and see!
On this, the highest tower of Ledjan, stands
A lance, and on the point of it is fixed
A golden apple. Take a bow and shoot
The apple. But there is a ring before,
Of finger's width – through that your shaft must pass!"

    Milosh did not await the herald's call.
At once he said: "My Tsar! May I now shoot
The apple through the ring of finger's width?"

    "You may, my own dear son!" the Tsar replied.

    So Milosh went beneath the shining tower.
He set an arrow to the golden cord;
He bent the bow and loosed the slender shaft –
It pierced the ring and struck the apple square,
Which fell, and Milosh took it to the Tsar.

    Great were the Tsar's rejoicings, and his gifts.

    A little time then passed, when yet again
A voice was heard to cry from Ledjan town:
"Now see, O Tsar! Beneath this shining tower
The King's two sons, two princes, have set out.
They lead with them three maidens, wondrous fair.
Of equal beauty all three maidens are,
And of all three the garments are the same.
Now choose which one of them is Roksanda!
And if you fail, or if your choice be false,
You nevermore shall leave this place alive,
Far less shall take the maiden as your bride!"

    When Stefan heard these words he called Todor
His old Vezir, and said: "You go and choose,
My good Todor, for you have seen her face."

    In grief Todor replied: "My lord, my Tsar!
I cannot, for I never saw her face;
For when they brought her to me it was night,
And in the darkness did I pledge your troth."

DUSHAN'S WEDDING

The Tsar then struck his hand upon his knee:
"Now, by the Living God, we are undone!
We had outwitted and out-championed them,
But now this girl will put us all to shame!"

Milosh Voyinovich heard this. He went
And stood before the Tsar. "My Tsar!" he said,
"Give me the task, for I shall pick her out!"
"Dear son, you may attempt it," said the Tsar,
"But shame it is to put our faith in you.
How can you truly choose Roksanda, whom
You never have set eyes upon, or known?"

Milosh Voyinovich replied to him
"My noble Tsar, you have no need to fear,
For, when I dwelt upon Shar's mountain-side
Twelve thousand sheep I watched. There, in a night
Perhaps three hundred lambs were born, and yet
Next day I knew each one, how like its dam –
Roksanda I shall know, how like her kin."

At that Stefan the Serbian Tsar cried out:
"Go, then, my very dearest son! – Go then!
And if you choose Roksanda, by God's grace,
My gift to you shall be Skenderia,[14]
That land, to have until your life be done!"

Milosh went forth on to the level plain,
And when he came to where the maidens stood
He pulled the shepherd's hat from off his head –
The overmantle from his shoulders shrugged –
His shimmering velvet garments then were seen.
The shining silver clasps upon his coat,
And golden greaves upon his legs, shone bright,
And Milosh stood in all his glory there,
As shines the burning sun in summer skies!
He spread his overmantle on the grass,
And on it strewed all kinds of jewellery –
Gold bracelets, rings, fine pearls, and precious stones.

– 17 –

And then he drew his sword, all glittering bright,
And, speaking to all three of them, he said:
"Whichever one of you is Roksanda,
To her alone this jewellery I give.
Let her now gather, in her skirts and sleeves,
These bracelets, rings, fine pearls, and precious stones.
But, if another touch, I swear to you
Upon my Faith, I'll chop her arms right off!"
    When those three lovely maidens heard, the two
Who stood each side looked quickly at the one
Who stood between them, with her eyes cast down
Upon the ground. Roksanda 'twas who stooped
To gather, in her skirts and silken sleeves,
The bracelets, rings, fine pearls, and precious stones.
The other two then fled, but Milosh ran
And caught them by the hand, and brought them back,
And then he led all three before the Tsar.
To him he gave Roksanda, and one more
To be a faithful maidservant for her;
The other maiden kept he for himself.

    The joyful Tsar kissed Milosh on the face,
But still he knew him not, or whence he came.

    The shining heralds went abroad and cried:
"O wedding-guests, make ready now each one!
For Tsar Stefan returns to Serbia."
    The wedding-guests made ready, and set forth,
The bride, Roksanda, in their company.
    And when they had but gone a little way
Milosh approached the Tsar, and said to him:
"My noble lord, O Tsar of all the Serbs!
There is an ogre still in Ledjan, called
Balachko. I know him of old, he me.
For seven years the King has nourished him
For just this task – to chase the wedding-guests

DUSHAN'S WEDDING

And seize Roksanda, and to take her back.
For that he now will send him after us.
This ogre, Lord Balachko, has three heads:
From one of them he vomits out blue flames,
And from another bursts an ice-cold blast!
But once those heads have belched their deadly winds
Balachko loses strength, and can be slain.
You go, my Tsar, and take your bride with you,
And I will here await Lord Balachko,
To stop him, and to put an end to him."

 The wedding-guests went on, upon the road;
The Tsar's bride, fair Roksanda, went with them.
But Milosh stayed upon the green hill-side,
And with him were three hundred men-at-arms.

 So, when the Serbs had left Ledjan, the King
Mihailo summoned Balachko to him:
"Balachko, our most faithful servant, say –
Are you to be relied upon? Will you
Pursue the wedding-party of the Tsar
To seize Roksanda, and to bring her back?"

 But my lord Balachko demurred; he asked:
"Your Majesty, of Ledjan noble King!
Who was that champion among the Serbs,
Who overcame in all the trials of strength?"

 But then the Queen of Ledjan answered him:
"Lord Balachko, our servant, mind your words!
There is no champion among the Serbs,
Except an unknown black Bulgarian,
A mere beardless boy, some shepherd lad."

 "That is no shepherd boy," Balachko said.
"That is Milosh Voyinovich, no less!
The Tsar himself does not know who he is,
But I know him of old, and he knows me."

 The Queen would hear no more, she ordered him:
"Lord Balachko, our servant, go! And seize

The maiden from the Serbs, and bring her back:
And she herself shall be our gift to you!"

Balachko then prepared his horse, and with
Six hundred Latin horsemen took the road,
And set off to pursue the Serbian host.

And as he came upon a green hill-side
A great dun horse was standing on the road,
Milosh Voyinovich astride its back.
As soon as he saw him, Balachko cried:
"Milosh, your end is come – abandon hope!"
And then he belched blue flame from his left mouth –
It reached Milosh, and charred his woollen coat.

When Balachko saw Milosh was not harmed
His other mouth blew forth an icy blast:
Milosh's horse in terror shied three times,
But Milosh was not hurt, and now he cried:
"It is for you to say farewell to hope!"

Then Milosh struck him with his golden mace –
But lightly struck, and yet he dashed him from
The saddle. Then he hurled his warrior's lance,
And pinned Balachko's body to the ground.
And after that he cut his three heads off,
And threw them in the nosebag of his horse.
Then he and his three hundred followers,
In furious charge, fell on the Latin band.
They killed them all, and cut off all their heads,
Then turning, set off to rejoin the Serbs.

When they arrived, Milosh approached the Tsar
And threw before him Balachko's three heads.
The Tsar gave him a thousand ducats' prize,
And all went on their way to fair Prizren.

But as they crossed the level plain of Kosovo,
Milosh approached the Tsar and asked his leave
To go instead to Vuchitern. He cried:

DUSHAN'S WEDDING

"May God be with you, dearest uncle mine:
My uncle Stefan, Tsar of all the Serbs!"

And then at last the Tsar became aware,
And knew he was Milosh Voyinovich.
"Milosh, my nephew dear, 'tis you!" he cried.
"How blessed is the mother who bore you!
How blessed is the uncle whom you've served!
Why did you not reveal yourself at first?
For on the way you must have suffered much
From poor lodging, hunger, cold, and thirst!"

My tale is told: misfortune lurks for him
Who ventures forth without his kith and kin.

2
Saint Peter and his Mother

Saint Peter took a walk to Paradise,
His mother followed, uttering great sighs:
"I'm old!" she cried, "Don't go so fast, my dear."
Said Peter: "There's no room for you in here!"

"For, down on Earth you made much rotten cloth –
And thus you spoiled your chances. God is wrath!
You cannot hope to gain Eternal Bliss
By selling shoddy as good stuff, like this."

Saint Peter took a walk ...

"In life, dear mother, wine was all your trade,
But, adding water, such great profit made
That you have forfeited Eternal Bliss –
You cannot water down such sins as this."

Saint Peter took a walk ...

"On Earth you made much money selling flour –
'Twas mostly ashes, though. At this Dread Hour
Too late it is to seek Eternal Bliss,
When you have cheated everyone like this!"

3
The Building of Ravanitsa

In Krushevats[1] did Tsar Lazar[2] decree
A great assembly of his noblemen.
They sat in order of their precedence,
And at their head was Tsar Lazar himself.
At his left hand sat Ivko of Konyits,
Beside him sat Zhivko of Homolye;
By Zhivko was the steward Bozhidar,
And next beside him sat Vuk Brankovich,[3]
And next to Vuk was Ivan Kosanchich,
And next to him was Milan Toplitsa;
Beside him sat Tsaritsa Militsa,
And next to her was Milosh Obilich.[4]
Militsa's brothers sat beside Milosh –
Young Petar and young Nikola they were,
The youngest and the frailest, Momir, too.

And at the Tsar's right hand in order sat
Old Yug-Bogdan the Venerable,[5] first,
With Banovich Strahinya[6] next to him,
And Stefan Musich[7] sat beside the Ban.
By Stefan sat Yovo Kuchainitsa,
By Yovo sat Petar Branichevats,
And after Petar all the other lords.

The steward Bozhidar was serving wine:
He tasted every glass before the Tsar,
And everybody drank the Tsar's good health.

The Tsar picked up a golden cup of wine –
He picked it up, but did not drink from it.
He pushed it to one side, and spoke aloud
To all the noblemen assembled there:
"Now look about you, noble Voivodas![8]
We sit together here and drink much wine:

We live like lords! – but carelessly neglect
Our bounden duty to posterity
To build memorials and monuments.
We have not built a church or monastery –
No bridges over rivers have we built,
No highways have we paved with lasting stone.
Before us, every Tsar and every Kral[9]
Has built some monument[10] that bears his name –
And finished it, or set the work in train.
Tsar Stefan built the tall white Dechani
Which stands so proudly in Metohiya;
(The building of it took a full twelve years).
His servant built the church in fair Prizren.
Kral Milutin erected tall Devich
Upon the level plain of Kosovo.
The famous George's Pillars Djuradj built –
Saint Petar's church besides, at Petrova.
Kral Simeon built Studenitsa church:
The Pridvornitsa church his servant built.
The two Mernyavchevichi built the church
At Yelitsa, upon the empty hills –
And put a roof of pine-wood over it.

But what have we done for posterity?
May God forgive us, nothing have we built!
And all the time there are two mines of gold:
One in Kopaonik's, one in Rudnik's hills!

Now, I shall build the finest monument!
I shall lay down a base of solid lead,
And build a frame of iron struts and beams,
And clad the frame entire with melted gold,
And cover all the walls with precious stones,
With small pearls intersprinkled over all.
So shall it shine – all men shall know it's mine!"

All sat in silence then. Not one said "Aye!"
And of that company not one said "No!"

THE BUILDING OF RAVANITSA

In lowly place sat Milosh Obilich.
His place was lowly, but his words were bold:
"My Tsar, you may! – you have the means at hand.
But, by the living God, I say to you
That these are not the times for such a thing.
The end draws near: these are the latter days
Before the terrible oppression comes,
When they will smash down your Memorial
Because of all its gold and precious stones.
The Turks will come and rip away the gold,
And they will break away the iron beams
And melt them down, and make them into rods
Which they will use to beat our people's backs.
The people then will curse you, and your soul,
And your Memorial will be no more.

Now hear me out, O Glorious Tsar Lazar!
For in the valley of the Resava[11]
– The Resava, which is within your realms,
Beneath the towering hills of Kuchaya –
There I have seen a pleasant place, my Tsar.
Build there your church, on Ravanitsa's plain![12]
Build it, my Tsar, as finely as you will.
Build it of stone, and nothing but white stone.
Inviolate then 'twill stand a thousand years –
Your Memorial – Ravanitsa Church!"

When Tsar Lazar the Glorious heard these words
He raised his cup to Milosh, and he cried:
"Well said! Good health, Milosh, my faithful knight!"
And then at last did Tsar Lazar drink wine.

The Glorious Tsar Lazar imposed a tax.
He laid the tax upon the Voivodas,
Who laid a tax upon each Kmet[13] and Knez,[14]
And on each chieftain and each ruling prince.
They gathered up a thousand artisans
And, to assist, a thousand labourers.

The master-builder Radé[15] was in charge.
Old Yug-Bogdan was Superintendant;
The brothers Yugovich[16] were Intendants.
The building was to take a full twelve years.
The day's wage was a ducat for skilled men
With, as gratuity, three pints of wine;
Days off for Saints Petka and Nedelya.
And so was Ravanitsa's church begun.

The Yugovichi were a pack of rogues.
The Tsar's materials they mostly sold;
The wages for the men they took themselves.
They broke the promises the Tsar had made –
They only paid a farthing as a wage,
And only gave a thimbleful of wine.
Saints Petka and Nedelya – no days off,
Nor yet Saint Ilia's Day, the Thunderer,
Nor the Lightning-bringer, Saint Maria.

The master-builder Rade, seeing this,
Called out to all his thousand artisans:
"Within the twelvemonth, finish all this work!"
He mounted then upon his fiery horse
And rode until he came to Krushevats.
Dismounting there, outside the walls, in haste,
He dropped the reins and left the horse to graze
While he himself went in to see the Tsar.
He found the Tsar in Council, but he went
Straight up to him, and made a humble bow;
With reverence he kissed his skirt and hand.
The Tsar sat on a gold-embroidered rug,
And Rade sat beside him, on his right.

The Tsar received him kindly, and he said:
"Rade, my architect! My precious one!
What of my church? Goes Ravanitsa well?
Come you to say the building's all in hand?

THE BUILDING OF RAVANITSA

Come you to tell me the foundation's laid?"
   Rade the master-builder answered him:
"My Tsar, I humbly beg, hear what I say!
The work is done: the building is complete.
For us it does not seem a holy place –
A prison, rather, for us working men!
My Tsar, you promised us fair wages, but
A farthing's all we've seen as a day's pay:
Gratuity – a thimbleful of wine.
Petka and Nedelya – no days of rest,
Nor yet Saint Ilia's or Maria's Days!"
   When Tsar Lazar the Glorious heard these words
He called before him Milosh Obilich.
"O Milosh, good and faithful servant, mount
That swift and strong grey horse of yours, and go
At once to Ravanitsa, to my church.
There, hang the brothers Yugovich, all nine!
But seize the old man, Yug-Bogdan, alive.
Wreak most dreadful agony upon him –
Gouge his staring eyes out of their sockets!
Wrench his teeth out, one by one, with pincers!
Rip his tongue out! Then, while he's still breathing,
Saw his suffering body into quarters!
Hang the pieces on four lofty branches!
– He who wonders, let him be astonished!
He who trembles, let him fear my anger!"

   And Milosh Obilich obeyed the Tsar.
He mounted on his swift and strong grey horse
And rode at once to Ravanitsa's church.
He seized the brothers Yugovich, all nine –
He tied their hands and bound their arms with rope;
He seized old Jug-Bogdan and bound him too.
   But, having bound them, Milosh sent them off
To Relya Krilatitsa[17] in Pazar.[18]
He sent a letter with them – thus it read:

– 27 –

"O Relya! Keep these people in your gaol,
But give them wine and rakia[19] to drink,
And feed them well with honey and sweet things."

Then Milosh mounted his grey battle-horse
And rode to Krushevats. When he arrived
He went into the palace of the Tsar
And to the council-chamber where the Tsar
Was sitting. Milosh humbly bowed, and said:
"It's done, my Tsar: I've hanged the lot of them!
I've hanged the brothers Yugovich, all nine.
I took the old man Yug-Bogdan alive,
And made him suffer dreadful agonies:
I gouged his staring eyes out of his head,
With pincers wrenched his teeth out, one by one;
I ripped his tongue out by the very roots,
And then I quartered him – chopped him in four,
And hung the pieces on four branches, high.
Those who wonder, let them be astonished!
Those who tremble, let them fear your anger!"

When Militsa, the Tsaritsa, heard this
She shrieked aloud and wailed in bitter grief:
"Oh why, my Tsar? Why, in the name of God?
Of nine sweet brothers could you not have spared
Just one, the youngest or the eldest, say,
To do you honour, and to stand by me?
Now look at me – bereft of all my kin!
Hear the crying of this anguished woman
As she swoops and falls like any swallow!"

And when the Glorious Tsar Lazar heard this
His heart was full of sorrow and remorse.
"O Milosh!" said the Tsar, "My faithful knight!
If only you had known, as you could not,
You might indeed have spared one out of nine,
Whether the youngest or the eldest one,
So that I now could have him by my side –

THE BUILDING OF RAVANITSA

With honey and sweet sugar nourish him,
Give him cool wine and rakia to drink,
Dress him in clothes of velvet and of silk.
If only that could be, then when my time
Is come to die, my Kingdom would be yours!"

Then Milosh Obilich addressed the Tsar:
"My noble Tsar! I beg you, hear me out.
I always have obeyed you faithfully
Till now, but this time I have disobeyed.
I have killed no one, whether young or old.
I bound them all, and sent them to Pazar,
Where Relya Krilatitsa is the lord.
I told Relya to hold them captive there,
But give them wine and rakia to drink,
And feed them well with honey and sweet things
Until, O Tsar, your anger might abate.
Now you may judge them as seems right to you.
But more than this, my Tsar, hear what I say –
They've built your church, and finely have they wrought.
Now let the men be paid their proper dues –
The wages that were promised to them all!"

The Tsar agreed with all that Milosh said,
And saw the men were paid their just reward.

Then was drawn up a noble cavalcade;
They mounted all on horses finely decked.
To Ravanitsa rode the Tsar in State
To view the church that he had ordered built.

And when the Tsar came within sight of it
He saw it, white and shining like the sun –
So brilliantly it shone, his startled horse
Was dazzled, and it reared and threw him off!

Because of that, the place he fell was called
"The Tsar's Great Bruise" – and so it is today!

4
Banovich Strahinya

Strahinyich Ban,[1] a noble man was he!
He was the Ban[2] of little Banska Town[3]
That nestles in the hills near Kosovo.
A nobler hero there has never been.

One morning early, when the Ban awoke,
He called his servants, and he said to them:
"Make haste, my servants all, and lose no time!
– Saddle up my battle-horse, my Djogo,
Harness him, and deck him in fine trappings.
Pull his girth as tight as you can make it!
For I, my children, have a mind to go
Upon a journey. Banska I shall leave,
And many weary hours must Djogo spend
Upon the road, for we shall travel far.
I yearn to see my relatives, my kin,
Who live in Krushevats,[4] that city fair.
There's my wife's father, dear old Yug-Bogdan,
And his nine sons, the brothers Yugovich;[5]
And dearly do I long to visit them."

The servants went to do as they were bid;
They saddled and bedecked Djogo the horse.
Meanwhile Strahinyich Ban prepared himself.
Fine clothes he wore, of velvet and brocade,
Of sumptuous fabrics, and of costly silk,
More bright than water: redder than the sun –
So dressed he, as befits a Serbian lord.
He mounted Djogo, his white battle-horse,
And set off on his way to Krushevats,
Where recently the Tsar had set his throne.

The old man Yug-Bogdan awaited him

As he approached: with him were his nine sons –
Those paladins, the brothers Yugovich.
Most kindly did they greet Strahinyich Ban
With words of welcome, and with fond embrace.
While servants took his horse and tended it
Yug-Bogdan led his son-in-law into
His castle hall, in the French manner built.
And there all sat on sofas and divans.
Servants and serving-maids were all at hand
To set before them food and bring them wine.
It was a goodly Christian company
That sat to drink cool wine in that fair hall!
Old Yug-Bogdan sat at the table's head;
At his right hand sat Strahinyich the Ban,
His son-in-law. Next to the Ban there sat
Yug-Bogdan's sons, nine brothers Yugovich.
The other gentlemen in order sat;
The youngest of them served their seniors.

    The wives of the nine brothers Yugovich
Were also there: they served their husbands and
They diligently served old Yug-Bogdan,
And specially his honoured son-in-law.
A steward served the wine to everyone:
He poured it from a massive golden jug
That held two gallons of the choicest wine.
O look! and see the delicacies there –
The meats, and fruits, and every sort of dish –
That company enjoyed a royal feast!

    For many days the Ban prolonged his stay.
For many days he revelled with his kin:
It was for him a joy to be with them.

    But the gentility of Krushevats
Became a burden, all throughout the day
Vying to importune old Yug-Bogdan:
"O mighty, venerable Yug-Bogdan!

Allow us, noble lord, to kiss your hem!
Permit us, sir, to kiss your princely hand!
We beg you, condescend to let us meet
Your gracious son-in-law, Strahinyich Ban!
And bring him to our houses and our halls,
That we may show him honour and respect!"

For all of them, their wish was satisfied,
And so, as many invitations came,
So many days were filled with visiting –
And so the Ban prolonged his stay yet more.

But see! All of a sudden all is changed!
There came one morning, when the sun was up,
A courier with a letter in his hand.
The letter came from Banska to the Ban,
'Twas from the aged mother of the Ban.
When it was brought to him he read it through.
The letter told of grim calamity,
And of his mother's suffering and tears:
"Strahinyich Ban, my son, where are you now?
The wine you drink in Krushevats is woe!
Woe is your wine, and misery your kin!
Now read this tale of terrible events!

Without a warning, suddenly, my son,
The Turks have come, in overwhelming force.
The Turkish King of Yedren,[6] in the east,
Has fallen on the land of Kosovo.
He sent his Vezirs and his Generals,
His grim and cruel representatives,
To pillage all the land of Kosovo.
They gathered up an army of the Turks,
And came to Kosovo and ravaged it.
Throughout the land they bear down everywhere.
The region of the waters have they seized –
Of both the rivers Lab and Sitnitsa –
The whole of Kosovo is under siege.

Bad news is still arriving, O my son,
Between the marble mines and maple woods,
And from the maple woods to Sazliya,
Where stands the bridge of arches on the stream;
From there to Zvechan and beyond, 'tis said,
To Chechan, to the very mountain-tops –
The Turkish hordes have struck all Kosovo!

The number of their men, my son, is great.
They have a hundred thousand under arms,
So it is said, raised by the noblemen
Who owe both suit and service to the King
Of Turkey, who has granted them their lands.
They ride on battle-horses, and although
They do not carry heavy weapons, yet
Each soldier has a sharp sword at his belt.

And more than that, the Turkish King has kept
At Yedren yet another army corps
Of regiments of fierce janissaries[7] –
Who are the King of Yedren's household troops –
Another hundred thousand, it is said.

And it is said that also, in reserve,
There is a third great army of the Turks,
Commanded by Tuku and Madjuku,
That will come, roaring and destroying all.

In all the Turkish hordes, there is one man
More terrible and cruel than the rest –
He is the renegade Vlah-Aliya.
He flouts the King's own orders, disregards
The Vezirs, and rampages on his own.
He takes no heed of what the army does.
The King commands a large and mighty force;
His horde of Turks infests the Earth like ants.
It was not meant that he should trouble us;
The Turkish army went to Kosovo.
But he defied the orders of the King

And, turning left, he came upon the road
That leads to Banska, our Banska, my son,
And bitter grief he brought to all of us.
He has destroyed our homes with burning fire –
The very ruins scattered – nothing's left.
Your faithful servants all have fled away.
He's harmed your mother, trampling her beneath
His horse's hooves, and breaking all her bones.
He's seized your own true love, your very wife!
And carried her away to Kosovo,
And had her in his tent throughout the night!

Among the ashes, son, I sit and weep,
While you are drinking wine in Krushevats.
Woe is your wine; now drink no more of it!"

And when the Ban had read the letter through
Great were his sorrow and his bitterness.
His cheeks were pale, his eyes were full of grief,
His great moustaches drooped down to his breast,
His aspect frowning and his visage dark,
His misery was there for all to see.
The tears flowed freely down his sombre face.

When Yug-Bogdan saw him, at break of day,
He flared with passion, like a living flame,
To see his son-in-law so sad, and cried:
"May God preserve us all, my precious son!
Why have you risen from your bed so soon?
What is it, son, that has so saddened you?
Why are your features darkened with such grief?
Has someone troubled you, or angered you?
Your brothers-in-law – have they laughed at you,
Insulted you, or spoken out of turn?
Or have their wives not served you properly?
Have we, your kin, failed you in any way?
Tell me, my son, what troubles you so much?"

Strahinyich Ban then spoke – his words poured out:
"O Yug-Bogdan, father-in-law so dear!
Your sons, my brothers-in-law, have been kind.
Their ladies have been very good to me,
In conversation, and in serving me.
Your family has failed me in no sense.
Here is the cause of my unhappiness –
This letter has arrived from Banska town,
My mother wrote it, and it's bitter news."

The Ban told Yug-Bogdan what he had learned –
How his estates had been destroyed by fire,
How all his servants had been put to flight,
How his own mother had been injured sore,
And how the Turk had carried off his wife:
"But, Yug-Bogdan, father-in-law so dear!
Although today she is my wedded wife,
She is your daughter born and bred as well –
The shame of it bears heavy on us both!

O Yug-Bogdan, father-in-law so dear!
When I am dead, I think you'll mourn for me;
Now feel for me, while I am still alive!
I humbly kiss your hand. I beg of you
To let me take the brothers Yugovich
– My brothers-in-law and your nine brave sons –
To come with me at once to Kosovo,
That I may seek him out, my enemy,
That cursed apostate, Vlah-Aliya,
Who has so cruelly enslaved my wife!

And do not be afraid, my father dear,
And worry for the safety of your sons;
As brothers-in-law they are dear to me,
For their appearance shall be wholly changed!
I shall disguise them all to look like Turks –
White turbans they shall wear upon their heads,
And on their backs green dolmans they shall wear,

And tightly-fitting trousers on their legs.
And at their belts they'll carry scimitars.
They'll look like Turkish soldiers, led by me.
   Call servants! Let them harness horses now,
And spread upon their backs the broad horsecloths,
Put saddles on, and pull the girths full tight!
As janissaries shall your sons appear,
And I shall carefully look after them,
For when we get to Kosovo, and there
Pass through the Turkish army's lines,
I'll play the part of officer, in front.
Your sons shall follow, as a proper troop
Of soldiers under my command. And if
We have to stop inside the Turkish camp –
If any of them stops or questions us,
In Turkish or Manovski, I don't mind,
I'll answer them most fairly in their tongue.
For I speak Turkish, and that dialect;
I understand the Arabs' language too,
And even some Albanian, at a pinch.
So shall I lead your sons to Kosovo,
And safely through the Turkish army there,
Until I come upon my enemy –
That cursed renegade Vlah-Aliya,
Who carried off my wife, my own true love!
Now let your sons be with me in my need!
Alone, my father, I may lose my life,
But, with your sons, I do not have to die
Or suffer wounds that may take long to heal."

   When Yug-Bogdan heard what the Ban had said
He flared up like a living flame, and then
In stern and measured tones he said to him:
"Strahinyich Ban, my dearest son-in-law!
Tomorrow, when you're calm, then will you see
What foolishness it is that you propose –

That I should let you take away my sons
To Kosovo: the Turks would slaughter them!
I will not hear another word of this!
I will not send my sons to Kosovo,
Although my daughter will be lost to me.

    Strahinyich Ban, my brave, foolhardy son!
Why do you let your mind be troubled so?
You know full well, my son, as all men know,
If she has spent a night inside his tent
And given herself to him in that night,
She can no longer be your own true love.
May God destroy her, for she is defiled!
Her love will be for him, not you, my son.
To Hell with her! – the Devil take her, then!
I'll find a better maid for you to wed.
I wish us to be friends for evermore
And in true amity to drink our wine –
But I'll not send my sons to Kosovo!"

    The Ban was filled with anger and with pain.
He did not call the servants, took no heed
Of groom or ostler, but he went alone
And unattended to the stables, where
His battle-horse Djogo awaited him.
Alone the Ban prepared and saddled him.
Alone the Ban pulled tight the surcingle.
Bridle and bit he fitted on, himself.
Alone he led him to the drinking-trough
Within the courtyard, and, when he had drunk,
Alone he led him to the mounting-block
Of marble stone. He patted Djogo's neck,
And looked upon his nine brothers-in-law,
Their eyes downcast; they could not meet his gaze.
A young man also stood there, Nemanyich –
He who had wed the sister of his wife –
His eyes downcast: he could not meet his gaze.

When the wine and rakia were flowing
All proclaimed themselves to be stout heroes –
Boasted to him – swore by God Almighty:
"Count on us, Strahinyich Ban! Whenever
You need help, we'll be your staunchest allies!"

But now, when danger threatens, see their shame!
'Twill be a hard and bitter thing to go
Friendless upon the road to Kosovo.

And when he saw not one of them would come,
Alone he rode out through the city gates
Of Krushevats, on to the level plain.
He turned to look back at the city fair –
His kin, perchance, might still yet change their minds:
Might yet repent of sending him alone
To face the grim task that awaited him
Upon the morrow, with no friend beside.
But, as he thought, there came into his mind
Remembrance of his greyhound, Karaman,
Whom he had left behind, and whom he loved
As much as he loved Djogo, his white horse.
He called aloud his name. Inside the town
The greyhound heard! He dashed out to the plain
And joined his master as he rode along.
So full of joy, the greyhound leaped and jumped,
And, as he ran, his golden collar flashed –
The Ban's heart now was filled with happiness.

The Ban rode on, on Djogo his white horse,
Across the fields and mountains on his way
To Kosovo. When he arrived he saw
The Turkish armies, rank on rank, spread out
Upon the plain, far as the eye could see.
Fear struck his heart, but then he prayed awhile
That God would give him courage for his task.
Then, straight into the Turkish camp he rode.

Throughout the Plain of Kosovo he rode.
From north to south, from east to west he rode.
He sought Vlah-Aliya, his enemy.
He searched in vain: he could not find the man.

  His quest led him to where Sitnitsa flows
Across the Plain of Kosovo, and there
Upon the bank he saw a wondrous sight.
There was a green pavilion standing there –
A marvellous pavilion, tall and wide,
With shining golden apples all bedecked
Which shone and glittered like the summer sun.
Before the tent, stuck in the ground, a lance,
And, tethered to the lance, a great black horse
Which stamped its hooves, and snorted as it fed –
A nosebag on its head of Turkish style.

  And when Strahinyich Ban saw this, he stopped
And stood awhile in thought. It crossed his mind
That he had come upon Vlah-Aliya's tent.
He drove his white horse forward, couched his lance,
And peered into the entrance of the tent
To see who was within.
                    But in that tent
Vlah-Aliya was not. Instead, there sat
Alone within, an ancient Turkish priest,
A dervish, with a white beard to his waist.
This scruffy fellow seemed a cheerful sort
– Drinking wine with gusto from a pitcher!
When his cup was empty, he refilled it –
This dervish saw the world through bloodshot eyes!

  And when the Ban saw him, he went inside
And greeted him the Turkish way: "Salaam!"
The drunken dervish eyed him for a while,
Then, to the Ban's astonishment, he said:
"I bid you welcome, Strahinyich, the Ban
Of little Banska town by Kosovo!"

The Ban flared up and angrily he cried:
"Ho, brother dervish, damn your mother's eyes!
You're rotten drunk, and talking drunken rot!
How dare you call a Turk by such a name?
I am a Muslim, not an infidel!
What's all this talk of some confounded Ban?
I am not Ban Strahinyich, but I am
An officer on duty for the King.
His horses have got loose and gone astray.
They've run among the Turkish regiments,
And every officer is chasing them
To round them up, and take them to the King.
If I should tell the King or his Vezirs
What nonsense you've been talking here today
You'll wish you'd never said it, you old fool!"

The dervish burst out laughing, and he said:
"My lord, Strahinyich Ban, I know you well!
But do not be upset. Had I today
Been on the hills of Golech, and had I
Looked down and seen you, in the Turkish camp,
I would have recognized you, and your steed,
And also Karaman, the hound you love
Still more than you love Djogo, your white horse.
I know you, Ban of little Banska town!
I know you by your forehead, and your brows,
I know you by your flashing eyes beneath,
And by those fine moustaches that you wear.
But do not be amazed, nor yet afraid.

For, long ago, I fell into your hands
When your patrolling sentries captured me
Upon the mountain heights of Suhara.
They brought me down to Banska, to your Court,
And you condemned me to imprisonment.
And so I languished in captivity;
For nine long years I was your prisoner.

The nine years passed, but, as the tenth drew near,
My Ban, you felt some mercy in your heart.
Your prison-keeper, Radé, turned the key
Of my cell door, and took me out of there
To stand before you in the prison-yard.
Do you remember? I remember well
The question that you asked, and what you said:
'You, my prisoner! You Turkish serpent!
Long years you have lain within my prison:
Can you pay a ransom for your freedom?'

And to your question this was my reply:
'I could do so. I have enough to pay
A ransom for my life, but only if
You will allow me to depart and go
To my own home, in my own fatherland.
I have a store of treasure there, not great.
As well as that, I have a large estate,
Awarded to me as gratuity;
I could collect the proper ransom price.
But you would never trust me to return
If you should let me journey to my home,
And how can I provide a guarantor?
I can but call upon Almighty God
To hold me to my promise to repay!'
My Ban, you trusted me! You let me go,
And sent me on my way to my own home.

But when I reached my fatherland, and came
To where my home was, and my own estate,
I found there nought but sorrow and despair.
There, in my home, the pestilence had struck;
My menfolk and my womenfolk – all dead!
My houses smashed: no part of them was left –
They broke them down and scattered all the stones,
And elder flowers were growing in the walls;
And my gratuity, my great estate –

All gone: my neighbours had drawn lots for it!
    And when I saw all doors were closed to me,
And no one there would help in any way,
– When wealth is gone, gone also are your friends –
I pondered long what I should do, and then
It came into my mind that I should go
To Yedren in the east to see the King.
I took post-horses, and to Yedren went,
And there I saw the King and his Vezir.
The Vezir saw that I had truly been
A soldier in the service of the King
And, for my service, I deserved a gift.
The Vezir gave me clothes, and this fine tent;
The King gave me that great black battle-horse,
A brightly-decorated sword besides;
They also gave me a Certificate
Of Military Service Well Performed.
    But now today, my Ban, you come to me
For payment of the debt I owe to you.
Alas, Strahinyich Ban, I have to say
That I've no longer got a penny-piece,
And you have come to die a senseless death
At Kosovo, amid this Turkish host!"

    The Ban then knew the dervish, who he was.
At once, dismounting, he embraced the man:
"By God, my friend, old dervish, have no fear!
The debt you owe I give you as a gift.
My brother, I'm not here to look for gold;
I do not seek repayment of your debt.
No! I am here to find Vlah-Aliya –
The man who has destroyed my very home
And snatched away and ravished my own wife.
Old dervish, tell me what you know of him –
Tell all you know about my enemy.
Now come, my friend, and let's embrace once more!

Do not betray my presence to the Turks
And make me fight my way through all of them!"

    The dervish, when they had embraced, then said:
"Strahinyich Ban, true Serbian lord you are!
Stronger than stone is my fidelity.
I know full well that you could draw your sword
And with it slaughter half the Turkish host –
But I will not betray you to the Turks,
Nor disregard the debt I owe to you
For, though you held me in captivity,
You let me have enough good wine to drink,
And gave me proper bread enough to eat,
And let me feel the sun upon my face,
And, with no surety, you set me free.
So I did not betray you, or forget.
I would have paid you, had I had the means.
There's nothing that you have to fear from me.
And, as for all the questions that you ask
About the mighty Turk Vlah-Aliya! –
That man has made his camp and pitched his tent
High up upon the Golech Mountain slopes.

    O Ban, hear me, and take my good advice –
Mount Djogo now and flee from Kosovo!
For otherwise you'll die a senseless death.
Alone, your bravery is not enough,
Nor are your strong right arm, your good sharp sword,
Nor yet your warrior's lance of tempered steel –
These things are not enough to save your life.
For when you come upon the man you seek,
Despite your weapons and your fine swift horse
You will be seized and brought before the Turk
By sentinels; and he will break your bones
And, while you live, tear out your staring eyes!"

    But Strahinyich the Ban just laughed, and said:
"Old dervish, brother, do not weep for me!

I shall prevail.   But this I ask of you –
That you do not betray me to the Turks."

  The ancient Turkish dervish answered him:
"Strahinyich Ban, hear what I say to you!
Stronger than stone is my fidelity.
– Even if you mount your fiery Djogo,
Even if you wield your flashing sabre,
Even if you slaughter half the army –
Never will I do you a disservice,
Nor will I betray you, now or ever!"

  In haste the Ban then mounted on his horse.
As he prepared to go, he turned and said:
"Old dervish, brother, there is one more thing.
You take your horse to water every day,
Both morn and evening, at the Sitnitsa.
Think carefully, and answer truthfully –
Where can I ford Sitnitsa's icy flood
Without my horse being stuck in a morass?"

  To which the ancient dervish made reply:
"O Serbian falcon! O Strahinyich Ban!
Your heroism and your noble steed
Shall part the waters: cross where'er you will!"

  The Ban then spurred his horse, and crossed the stream;
He urged him on toward the towering hills
Of Golech, far across the level plain.
He rode alone, but over him the sun
Blazed down upon the Plain of Kosovo
And on the army of the Turkish King.

  Now see Vlah-Aliya the Mighty there!
Up on the hill, the Turk was in his tent
Asleep. It was the custom of the Turk
To sleep until the sun had warmed the day.
So Vlah-Aliya closed his eyes and dreamed
Of how he had seduced the Ban's own wife,

BANOVICH STRAHINYA

Of his delight in her, his captive slave.
And so he slept, his head upon her lap!

    And as she held Vlah-Aliya asleep
The wife of Ban Strahinyich looked outside
The tent, upon the Plain of Kosovo,
Where lay the Turkish army all encamped.
With idle eyes she gazed upon the tents;
She watched the horses and the soldiers there.

    Then, suddenly, her eyes were filled with dread
For there, upon the plain beneath the hill
She saw a man approaching on his horse,
And searching with his eyes all round about.
She shook the Turk: she hit him with her hand –
She struck him with her palm upon the cheek –
She struck him hard – she roused him, and she cried:
"Vlah-Aliya the Mighty! O my lord!
Wake up! Wake up! Get up, and stand to arms!

    Quickly! Buckle on your battle-harness,
Clip your shining sabre on your waist-belt!
Look! See! Strahinyich Ban is coming here –
And he will cut your head off with his sword,
And he will dig my eyes out with its point!"

    Vlah-Aliya looked up, his eyes ablaze.
He looked at where she pointed, then he laughed:
"Strahinyova[8] my heart, my dearest love!
Be not so nervous of that infidel:
You start at shadows, there's no cause for fear!
When you're with me in Yedren, even there
You'll still imagine that the Ban is near!
That man approaching's not Strahinyich Ban:
He is a Turkish officer, no more.
No doubt the King, or Mehmed his Vezir,
Has ordered him to bring me some complaint
That I have caused disturbances, or such,

And telling me to come before his court.
The King's vezirs are sore afraid of me –
They fear that I will strike them with my sword!
Now, you can see with your own eyes, my dear,
That there's no need for you to fear that man.
When he comes up to me I'll draw my sword
And whip the silly fellow with the flat –
They'll not send further messengers to me!"

The frantic woman cried out urgently:
"Vlah-Aliya the Mighty! O my lord!
Can you not see? Do your eyes not tell you?
That is no Turkish officer who comes –
It is my husband, Strahinyich the Ban!
I know him by his forehead, and his brows;
I know him by his flashing eyes beneath,
And by those great moustaches that he wears!
And that is Djogo, his white battle-horse,
And that is his brown greyhound, Karaman!
My lord! This is no time for pleasantries!"

These words struck home. The Turk Vlah-Aliya,
Now fully roused, leapt up upon his feet:
His battle-harness buckled on, and thrust
Two pointed daggers in his belt. He took
His shining sword and clipped it on, and then
He checked the harness of his great black horse.

Meanwhile, the Ban approached at steady pace,
With caution, lest some treachery befall.
No greeting of "Good morning!" did he give;
He uttered not the Turkish word "Salaam!"
With no polite civilities, he cried:
    "So there you are, you swine! You bastard Turk!
You apostate! You good-for-nothing scum!
My home and property you have destroyed –
My family and kin you have enslaved –

My wife you've foully ravished in your tent –
Now stand and fight – a duel to the death!"

Vlah-Aliya shook himself, and then moved fast.
He took two bounds – the first towards his horse,
And with the second bound he mounted it,
And gathered up the reins between his hands.
Strahinyich Ban launched his attack at once.
He spurred his horse and charged towards the Turk.
He hurled his warrior's lance to pierce his breast –
And so between these titans battle joined.
But mighty Vlah-Aliya raised his hand
And caught the heavy lance while yet it flew.
Then he it was who spoke. He shouted out:
"You bastard infidel, Strahinyich Ban!
What idiotic dream has turned your head?
Lo! I am not some ancient Serbian crone
That you can frighten just by shouting threats.
No! I am the mighty Vlah-Aliya,
Who fears no king, no vezir, and no man!
There is no mightier warrior than I
In all the armies of the Turkish king,
Whose armies are as numberless as ants
That swarm on summer days amongst the grass –
And you, poor fool, think you can challenge me!"

So spake the Turk. He hurled the heavy lance
That he held in his hand. His aim was true.
Now only God can save Strahinyich Ban! –
But he rode Djogo, that great battle-horse,
And, as the lance came hissing through the air,
Djogo dropped instantly upon his knees!
The lance flew overhead and fell to earth
Behind Strahinyich on the stony ground,
And there the lance was shattered in three parts,
From pommel to the handgrip, to the tip.

Their lances broken, they abandoned them
And took their spiked bludgeons in their hands.
First Vlah-Aliya struck Strahinyich Ban
A blow so hard that it unseated him
And left him sprawling on his horse's neck.
Now only God can save Strahinyich Ban!
But he rode Djogo, that great battle-horse,
– The like of which you will not see today,
Whether among the Serbs, or yet the Turks –
And Djogo swung his head with massive strength
To stop his master's fall, and jerked him back
Into the saddle! Then Strahinyich Ban
Struck back. He struck Vlah-Aliya the Turk:
He struck with all his might. He still could not
Unseat him, but he forced the Turk's black horse
To buckle at the knees and sink right down
Upon the ground. So mighty were their blows
That all the spikes upon their bludgeons broke.
They drew their swords, and each began to cut
And thrust and parry, clashing as they fought.

Now see Strahinyich Ban, and see his sword –
That mighty sword he wields in his strong hand!
Two master-swordsmiths worked to make that sword,
Two skilful farriers, with three men to help.
They took the steel and worked a week of days
To forge, to temper, and to sharpen it.
And now Vlah-Aliya swung his sharp sword
To cut the head off Strahinyich the Ban,
But he was ready: sword-blade met sword-blade,
And see! –Vlah-Aliya's sword is snapped in half!

The Ban saw this and, filled with fierce joy,
He struck and struck again, to left and right –
He aimed to slice his head off with his sword,
Or deal his hands or arms decisive wounds.

BANOVICH STRAHINYA

The Turk closed in: they grappled knee to knee.
To save his head and hands the Turk fought on –
With his half-sword he parried the Ban's cuts,
And so he guarded well his head and hands.
And then he broke the Ban's sword: half the blade
Was snapped right off, and dropped upon the ground.
And, as they fought on, trading cut for cut,
Each broke off pieces of the other's sword
Until each held a hilt and nothing more!

Each one threw down the remnants of his sword
And each dismounted from his battle-horse.
Each seized the other by the throat, and so
They grappled, like two dragons making war
Upon that field, upon that mountain-side.
 They fought, upon that summer's day, till noon.
They foamed with sweat: the Turk's as white as snow,
The Ban's all white, but tinged with red as well,
For blood bespattered all his clothes and shoes.

The Ban grew tired, and shouted to his wife:
"My wife! My lady! For the love of God!
Why do you stand and watch in idleness?
Make haste! Pick up a piece of broken sword,
And strike the Turk with it – or else strike me!
Decide, my love, who is most dear to you!"
 The Turk then shouted to her in his turn:
"Strahinyova my darling, dearest heart!
Do not strike me, but strike Strahinyich Ban!
For you will nevermore be dear to him –
He will for ever hold you in disdain
And bitterly reproach you, night and day,
For that you slept with me inside my tent.
But I will ever give you my true love.
I'll take you home to Yedren, that fair town,
And thirty maids shall serve you constantly,

And you shall dress in clothes of precious silk,
And honey and sweet sugar shall you eat,
And you shall be bedecked with golden coins
Right from your head down to your very feet.
My precious one – now! Strike Strahinyich Ban!"

The woman's heart was easily seduced.
She leapt up like a thing possessed, and ran
To gather up a piece of broken sword.
She wrapped a silken handkerchief around
So that she should not hurt her pure white hands,
And then she ran to them. She slashed and stabbed –
She did not strike the Turk Vlah-Aliya:
It was Strahinyich Ban that she attacked –
Strahinyich Ban, her husband and her lord!
She slashed and tore the feathered cap he wore,
And under it the turban round his head.
She ripped through both the turban and the cap,
And with the jagged shard she cut his head,
And blood flowed down upon his noble face –
It ran into his eyes: he could not see.

His heart was filled with fear that he was now
To meet a senseless and ignoble death.
As he despaired, a thought came to his mind,
And then from his pale throat he called aloud –
He called aloud the name of Karaman,
The brown greyhound that he had trained to hunt.
Again he shouted, louder: "Karaman!"
The hound raced up to them, and with his jaws
He seized the woman, and he held her fast!

The woman's heart was craven, full of fear;
She was afraid of dogs, as women are.
She dropped the piece of sword upon the ground
And shrieked aloud: her cries were heard afar.

In vain she beat the hound about the ears,
And struggled, as he dragged her from the scene.

And now it was the Turk who knew despair:
In grief he saw the woman dragged away,
And saw the deadly peril he was in.
The Ban, though, felt himself recovering,
And as his strength returned his heart grew strong.
He struck, and struck again, with mighty blows,
Until he beat the Turk down to his knees.
So great his passion, and so great his wrath
He recked not that no weapon was to hand
But, opening his mouth, he seized the Turk's
Bare throat between his teeth, and ripped it out!
He killed him, as a hungry wolf a lamb!

The Ban leapt up, and shouted to his hound
To loose the woman whom he still held fast;
He shouted twice before the hound obeyed.
At once the woman tried to flee downhill –
She wanted to seek refuge with the Turks.
But Strahinyich Ban would not let her go.
He ran and stopped her: seized her by the hand,
And led her back to where his white horse stood.
He patted Djogo's neck, then mounted him;
He made his wife mount too, and sit behind.
And then the Ban made haste to leave that place.
He rode directly, by a slanting route,
To get away from there, and to avoid
The Turkish army spread about the plain.
He rode to Krushevats to join his kin.

As he approached the town, old Yug-Bogdan
And his nine sons came out to welcome him.
They all embraced him, and they kissed his cheeks,
And eagerly they asked how he had fared.
But when old Yug-Bogdan perceived that he

Was wounded in the head, his cap all torn,
The tears flowed down his face, and he burst out:
"Woe to our kingdom! Now we see, in truth,
The Turkish king has warriors strong enough
To wound my very son-in-law, who is
Himself a hero of surpassing might."

   The Ban's nine brothers-in-law were afraid
For him, but Strahinyich the Ban cried out:
"Dear father-in-law, do not grieve for me!
And you, my brothers-in-law, do not fear!
It was no hero in the Turkish ranks
Who tried to kill me, and who wounded me
While I was doing battle with the Turk.
My father, venerable Yug-Bogdan,
I'll tell you who it was who did this thing –
That woman there, your daughter, and my wife!
My own dear wife it was who wounded me –
Who would not take my part, but helped the Turk!"

   Yug-Bogdan shouted out in furious rage:
"My sons! My sons! Now draw your sharpened knives
And cut the bitch in pieces where she stands!"

   The brothers Yugovich all drew their knives
And made to kill their sister.
                         But the Ban
Prevented them from doing it. He cried:
"My brothers-in-law, do you have no shame –
And will you kill a woman with your knives?
O my heroic brothers, where were you,
And where were all your sharpened knives and swords,
When I went all alone to Kosovo?
You were not there, to do heroic deeds
Against the Turks, when I was in sore need!
I will not let you kill your sister now:
Myself, I could have killed her, without you!

Now you, my kin, are dead men in my sight:
No longer will I drink cool wine with you.
And as for her, see! – I have spared her life."

  Of all the heroes that have ever been,
One nobler than the Ban was never seen.

BALLADS OF
THE BATTLE OF KOSOVO

5
Tsar Lazar and Tsaritsa Militsa

Tsar Lazar[1] sat at supper, and with him
Sat Militsa his wife, the Tsaritsa.
And Tsaritsa Militsa said to him:
"Tsar Lazar, Golden Crown of Serbia!
Tomorrow you will go to Kosovo,[2]
Leading the kings and all the Serbian host –
Leaving us womenfolk alone, good Tsar,
With no stout knight to act as messenger
To carry news to you at Kosovo,
And bring us letters back to tell of you.
Among your armies my nine brothers are –
Those famous nine, the brothers Yugovich.[3]
Do not take all of them: leave one behind –
One brother for his sister still to hold!"

And Lazar, Tsar of all the Serbs, replied:
"O Tsaritsa Militsa, dearest wife!
But say which brother you do love the most,
And he shall stay with you in this fair hall."

"My lord, leave Boshko Yugovich with me!"
Said Militsa. And Lazar answered her:
"Militsa! Tsaritsa! My dearest wife!
Tomorrow, then, when dawn brings forth the day
And when the sun has warmed the morrow's morn,
Then will the city gates be opened wide.
Go to the gate-tower; wait beside the road.
Then through the gates of Krushevats[4] will pass
The Serbian battalions under arms.
And when the horsemen come, each with his lance,
Before them Boshko Yugovich will ride,
Bearing the sacred flag of Christendom.
Tell him that, with my blessing, he may give

The holy flag to whom he will, and stay
With you, at home, and not go to the war."

So when the gates were opened, with the dawn,
The Tsaritsa Militsa stood there, while
The Serbian legions under arms passed through.
See! in the van, the Lancers! At their head
Rides Boshko Yugovich, all mailed in gold,
And carrying the sacred Christian flag –
Enfolding man and horse, so vast it is!
That banner, all bestrewn with golden orbs;
Above each orb, emblazoned, a gold cross,
And from the staff hang flowers of pure gold,
Which sway and tap his shoulders as he rides!
So Christendom's flag flew, in Boshko's hand.

And Tsaritsa Militsa went to him;
She held the reins, and stopped his sorrel horse.
She wound her arms about her brother's neck
And quietly she whispered in his ear:
"O Boshko Yugovich, my brother dear!
The Tsar has given you to me: he says
You shall not go to war at Kosovo,
But says that, with his blessing, you may give
The holy flag to whom you will, and stay
With me in Krushevats, that one may live –
That I may have one brother still to hold!"

But Boshko would not heed her words. He said:
"My sister, go! – and bide in your fair hall.
I will not turn aside and stay with you,
Nor pass the sacred flag to any man,
Were Krushevats itself to be the price.
For never shall it be that men may say:
'See! There's that coward Boshko Yugovich,
Who dared not take the field at Kosovo,
Who dared not shed his blood for Jesus' sake,
Who would not give his life for Christendom!'"

SERBIAN EPIC BALLADS

He spurred his horse, and passed on through the gates.
And after him there came old Yug-Bogdan,[5]
And seven of the brothers Yugovich.
Of them she stopped each one – not one would stay;
Not one of them would listen to her pleas.

A little more time passed and then there came,
Upon his charger, Voyin Yugovich.
His duty was to lead the Tsar's remounts –
Those steeds, all blanketed in cloth of gold.
Militsa ran to him and stopped his horse.
She flung her arms around her brother's neck,
And whispered, as she had to all the rest:
"O Voyin Yugovich, my brother dear!
The Tsar has given you to me – he gives
His blessing. You must choose another squire
To lead the remounts. Only you must stay
With me in Krushevats, that you may live –
That I may have one brother still to hold!"

But Voyin would not heed her words. He said:
"My sister, go! – and bide in your fair hall.
I would not turn aside and stay with you,
Nor would I pass my trust to any man,
E'en though I knew it led me to my death.
Now, to the level plain of Kosovo
I go, to shed my blood for Jesus' sake,
And, with my brothers, die for Christendom!"
He shook the reins, and passed on through the gates.

Tsaritsa Militsa could bear no more:
Senseless she fell, and on the cold stones lay.

Just then the Tsar, Lazar himself, rode by
And saw his own Tsaritsa lying there.
The tears sprang forth and flowed upon his cheeks.
He turned his head aside – looked left and right.
But then he called his steward, Goluban,

– 58 –

Who rode beside him on a fine white horse:
"My trusty servant Goluban, dismount!
Look to my lady – lift her gently up,
And take her to a peaceful place within.
Now may God's blessing be on you and her:
You shall not come with me to Kosovo,
But here shall stay with her in Krushevats."

   When Goluban heard what the Tsar had said
He wept, and tears flowed down his pallid cheeks;
But he obeyed the Tsar. Dismounting from
His battle-horse, he picked the lady up
And took her to a peaceful room inside.

   But in the servant's heart there was no peace,
That he alone should not go to the war.
He fled away to where his horse was stood
And, mounting, turned and rode to Kosovo.

   At last the morrow's morn brought forth the day.
Then, from the level plain of Kosovo
Two flying ravens came, as dark as night.
They flew to Krushevats, and came to earth
Outside the very palace of the Tsar.
One croaked. The other spoke aloud: "Is this
The palace of the glorious Tsar Lazar?
Who is within? Is there, then, no one here?"
But from inside that place no voice was heard.

   Within, Militsa heard the ravens' cry.
She went out from the hall and spoke to them:
"May God be with you, ravens, dark as night!
Whence are you come? And yesterday where flew?
Come you from Kosovo? And did you see
Upon the field two mighty armies there?
And did the armies meet – did battle rage?
O ravens, say! – which army triumphed there?"

   The two black ravens spoke, and answered her:
"God be with us, Tsaritsa Militsa!

Aye, yesterday we were at Kosovo.
We saw the two great armies, all arrayed
For battle, and we saw them meet and fight.
So terribly they clashed – both kings are dead.
Now, of the Turkish army some still live,
But of the army of the Serbs, not one
Is left – not one, but's wounded unto death."

   So spake the ravens. After which there came
Milutin, faithful steward of the Tsar.
He held his broken right hand in his left.
From seventeen great wounds the blood poured out
All on his horse, which staggered in the gore.
And when Militsa saw him she cried out:
"Milutin! What is this? For pity's sake –
Have you betrayed your Tsar at Kosovo?"

   But Milutin could barely speak. He said:
"I beg you, O my lady, help me down.
For God's sake, bring cold water for my wounds,
And bring red wine for me to drink: the pain
Has conquered me, and I can bear no more."

   Militsa helped Milutin from his horse;
She brought cold water, and she bathed his wounds,
She brought red wine, and poured it out for him.
And so awhile he lay, recovering.

   When he was eased, and once again could speak,
Tsaritsa Militsa cried: "Milutin!
O faithful servant! – what of Kosovo?
Where are you now, my glorious Prince Lazar?
Where are you now, dear father Yug-Bogdan?
Where are you now, nine brothers Yugovich?
Where are you now, Milosh the Voivoda?[6]
Where are you now, Vuk Brankovich the Brave?[7]
Where are you now, Banovich Strahinya?"[8]

   And in low tones Milutin answer made:
"My lady, fallen, all, at Kosovo!

LAZAR AND MILITSA

The Tsar, Lazar the Glorious, is dead.
But round him many broken weapons lie
By those who bore them in defence of him.
There are more Serbian dead than Saracen,
For every Serb strove mightily to guard
His noble master, glorious Tsar Lazar.
Old Yug-Bogdan lies there. He met his end
At once, as soon as battle had begun.
Of all your brothers, Yugovich, eight fell:
Each strove to save his brother, till at last
But one was left – Boshko, who bore the flag.
Christ's banner yet streamed over Kosovo!
He hurled himself upon the Turks, who fled
In droves, as flee soft doves before a hawk.
At last he fell. Banovich Strahinya
Fell fighting, wading to his knees in blood.
My lady, Voivoda Milosh is dead.
He lies beside Sitnitsa's icy stream[9] –
But many Turks lie by him, for he slew
Murat their chief, beside twelve thousand more.
Upon his father may God's blessing be –
Milosh shall be remembered in this land
Whenever tales are told by Serbian folk,
As long as Mankind is, and Kosovo!
    But do not ask me of Vuk Brankovich.
Cursed be his tribe! Cursed be they who spawned him!
Cursed be his children and his progeny!
For he betrayed his Tsar at Kosovo,
And, with twelve thousand horsemen, fled the field."

6
Stefan Musich

In Maidan, that fair town with silver walls,[1]
Sat Stefan Musich,[2] drinking good red wine
Within his beautiful and noble hall;
Vaistina, his servant, filled the cups.
And when Stefan had drunk his fill, he said:
"Vaistina, my servant good and true!
The time has come for me to take my rest.
You eat your supper, drink your fill of wine,
Then go outside and stand before the hall.
Look upwards to the clear and cloudless sky –
See if the moon is on the wane, and if
The Day-star's shining brightly in the east.
If so, the time has come for us to go
To Kosovo's broad level plain, to keep
Our promise to Lazar, our noble Prince.[3]
For you know well, my friend, that we have sworn
A sacred, solemn oath to follow him
And, when we swore, he laid upon whomso
Should fail to keep his oath this dreadful curse:
 'If any Serb, or man of Serbian birth,
Or any man of Serbian kith or kin,
If any such a man comes not with me
To battle on the Field of Kosovo –
Never shall he know a son or daughter.
Whatsoever he may touch shall wither:
Vineyard, field of wheat – his sweat and labour
Fruitless, and his generation barren!' "
 So saying, Stefan Musich went to bed.

 Vaistina obeyed his master's words.
He ate his supper, drank his wine, and then
He went outside his master's noble hall

And looked up to the cloudless sky. The moon
Was on the wane, and in the east there shone
The Day-star, bright and clear. And then he knew
The time had come for them to journey to
The fair and level plain of Kosovo,
To join their Prince, according to their word.

   He went down to the stables, and brought out
Two battle-horses, and he saddled them
And harnessed and caparisoned them both –
One was his master's, and the other his.
He led them to the palace gate, and there
He took his master's silken battle-flag.
Twelve crosses were emblazoned on that flag,
With every cross embroidered in pure gold,
And in their midst the icon of Saint John,
The patron saint of Stefan's family.
He leaned the banner on the courtyard wall
And then he went inside and up the stairs
That he might wake his master from his sleep.

   When he was by his master's bedroom door
The wife of Stefan Musich came to him.
She clasped him eagerly – she kissed his cheek –
She warned him of her dark presentiment:
"God be with you, Vaistina, my dear!
In God's name, and Saint John's most holy name –
A faithful servant you have always been;
I swear, my very brother you shall be.
Do not awake my husband, I implore!
In misery I dreamed an awful dream:
I saw two peregrines that flew, and led
A flock of doves above this noble hall.
I dreamed I saw them fly to Kosovo
And into Murat's camp,[4] and there they fell,
And when they fell they did not rise again.
It is your destiny that I have seen;

Take heed of what I say: you both will die!"
　　Vaistina the servant answered her:
"Dear lady! Sister! That I can not do.
He is my lord: I can not break my faith
With him who is my master, and is yours.
You are not bound, my lady, as are we,
By that great oath that we have sworn, for breach
Of which our Prince pronounced this dreadful curse:
'If any Serb, or man of Serbian birth,
Or any man of Serbian kin, comes not
To battle on the Field of Kosovo –
Whatsoever he may touch shall wither;
Vineyard, field of wheat, he'll never reap them,
Nor shall he be blessed with son or daughter;
Fruitless, barren, all his sweat and labour!'
And that is why, dear lady, I can not
Be faithless to my master and to yours."

　　He left the lady then and went into
His master's bedroom, and awakened him:
"Wake up, good master! for the time has come
For us to take the road to Kosovo."
　　Then Stefan Musich rose and stood upright.
He washed his face, and donned his knightly garb,
And buckled on his sword, so finely wrought.
Then Stefan took a goblet of red wine
And drank, in honour of his Holy Saint:
"Safe journey!" and "Blest be the Holy Cross!"
As he was wont to do, whenever he
Set out upon a journey, or returned.
　　Then outside to the courtyard did he go.
The two great battle-horses waited there.
The lord and servant mounted, each his own.
The gold-encrusted banners were unfurled,
The drums they beat, the trumpets sounded out –
And Stefan Musich led his host to war.

STEFAN MUSICH

And as a pale dawn lit the way for them
Upon the level plain of Kosovo,
They came upon a maid of Kosovo.
She bore two golden pitchers in her hands,
Both empty, and she held beneath her arm
A nobleman's white silken head-dress, with
A spray of feathers stitched upon the cloth.
Those feathers were of silver at the base,
Their stems were golden, and their tips were pearls.

And Stefan Musich gently said to her:
"God's blessing be upon you, my dear child!
Have you been straying near a battlefield?
Where did you get that lordly silken cap?
Give it to me, my dear, that I may look
More closely at the emblem that it bears.
It has been fortunate for you and me
That we have met. Fear not – I mean no harm!"

The maid of Kosovo made straight reply:
"May God be with you, noble Voivoda!
I've not been straying near a battlefield.
My mother woke me early, for it is
Our habit to draw water from the stream.
But, to Sitnitsa's waters[5] when I came
I found the river troubled and in flood.
There floated on it horses, and dead men,
And there were Turkish turbans too, and scarves,
And Serbian embroidered silken caps.
This one was floating near the river bank,
I waded in and got it from the stream.
At home I have a younger brother, and
I took this pretty feathered cap for him.
I'm only little – please don't scold me, sir!"

She gave the cap of silken cloth to him,
And Stefan Musich recognised its badge –
The spray of golden feathers, and the pearls –

– 65 –

And when he saw it closely, then he knew
Whose it had been. The tears flowed down his cheeks.
He smote his knee: he ripped the scarlet cloth,
And broke the golden buttons on his sleeve.
"Dear God!" he cried, "How bitter is my grief!
I was not there, beside my noble Prince,
When battle joined: wherefore I stand accursed
For breaking that great oath I swore to him!"

He gave the silken cap back to the girl.
He felt inside his pocket, and he found
Three yellow ducats, which he gave to her.
"Take these, young maid of Kosovo," he said,
"Now I must hasten also to the war,
For Jesus' sake, and in the name of Christ.
If God allows that I should come again
Upon this path, you shall have better things.
But if it must be that I perish there,
Remember me by this small gift, my dear."

He spurred his horse. He galloped through the stream
And plunged into the battle. So at last
Did Stefan Musich fight at Kosovo.
He battled with three pashas – them he slew –
But as he fought the next he met his end.
Vaistina, his faithful servant, fell
Beside him. And there perished on that field
The full twelve thousand warriors that he led.
And also on that field our Prince was slain.

And in that place where fell our righteous Prince
The earthly realm of Serbia was lost.

7
The Maiden of Kosovo

She rose at dawn, a maid of Kosovo,
She rose at dawn, upon a Sunday morn,
A Sunday morn, before the day's great heat.
And of her flaxen shirt she rolled the sleeves
Up to the elbows of her pure white arms.
She carried wheaten bread upon her back,
And in her hands she bore two golden jugs;
In one of them was water, pure and cool,
And in the other jug was good red wine.

The maiden went upon the level plain
Of Kosovo, upon the battlefield:
The field of battle of our noble Prince –
Among the fallen warriors, and the blood.
And when she found a warrior yet alive
She washed his wounds with water, pure and cool,
And gave him wine to drink and bread to eat,
As though she served the sacraments to him.

And, in her wandering, she came upon
A fallen hero, Pavle Orlovich,
The standard-bearer of our noble Prince.
She found him still alive, but wounded sore:
His right arm had been struck off by a sword,
And his left leg was severed at the knee.
Within his chest his slender ribs were smashed;
His pallid lungs were gaping through the wound.
She moved him from a reeking pool of blood.
She washed his wounds with water, pure and cool,
She gave him wine to drink and bread to eat,
As though she served the sacraments to him.

SERBIAN EPIC BALLADS

And when his heart had fluttered into life
Did Pavle Orlovich speak thus to her:
"Dear sister, gentle maid of Kosovo!
What great and dread misfortune do you come
To find, amid the blood of fallen men?
Whom seek you on the battlefield, my child?
A brother or a cousin, may it be,
Or him who fathered you by earthly love?"

The maid of Kosovo replied to him:
"Dear brother, whosoever you may be!
In truth, I have not come to find my kin.
No brother and no cousin do I seek,
Nor yet the man who fathered me on earth.
You know that Prince Lazar,[1] when battle loomed,
Commanded that his armies should receive
Communion at Samodrezhna church.
Three weeks it was, with thirty priests, before
The Serbian armies all were sanctified.
The last to come were three great noblemen:
Of them, Milosh the Voivoda[2] was first,
And after him was Ivan Kosanchich;
The third of them was Milan Toplitsa.

And I was there, beside the church's door,
When Milosh, mighty Voivoda, came by –
A glorious hero in the world of men –
So great his sword, it trailed upon the ground,
His silken cap with feathers all bedecked.
He wore a lordly fine-embroidered cloak;
A silken kerchief was about his neck.
He turned to me and looked upon my face,
Then from his shoulders did he take his cloak.
He took it off – he gave the cloak to me
And said: 'Fair maiden, take this cloak of mine!
So may you have a memory of me,
Both by this cloak, and by the name I bear.

THE MAIDEN OF KOSOVO

For now I go, my precious one, to die
Among the legions of my noble Prince.
My dearest maiden, pray to God above
That I return alive from whence I go,
And also that good fortune come to you;
For you shall marry Milan Toplitsa,
Who is my brother in the sight of God.
Both he and I are true blood-brothers sworn
Before our Heavenly Father and Saint John,
And I shall be your Witness when you wed.'

And after him came Ivan Kosanchich –
A glorious hero in the world of men –
So great his sword, it trailed upon the ground,
His silken cap with feathers all bedecked.
He wore a lordly fine-embroidered cloak,
A silken kerchief was about his neck,
And on his hand a golden wedding-ring.
He turned to me and looked upon my face.
He took the golden wedding-ring; he took
It off his hand. He gave the ring to me
And said: 'Sweet maiden, take this ring of mine!
So may you have a memory of me,
Both by this ring, and by the name I bear.
For now I go, my precious one, to die
Among the legions of my noble Prince.
My dearest maiden, pray to God above
That I return alive from whence I go,
And also that good fortune come to you;
For you shall marry Milan Toplitsa,
Who is my brother in the sight of God,
Both he and I are true blood-brothers sworn
Before our Heavenly Father and Saint John;
And I shall be the Best Man when you wed.'

And after him came Milan Toplitsa –
A glorious hero in the world of men –
So great his sword, it trailed upon the ground,
His silken cap with feathers all bedecked.
He wore a lordly fine-embroidered cloak,
A silken kerchief was about his neck,
And in his hands a veil of cloth-of-gold.
He turned his head and looked upon my face.
He took the veil of cloth-of-gold he held –
He took the veil, and handed it to me
And said: 'Dear maiden, take this veil of mine!
So may you have a memory of me,
Both by this veil, and by the name I bear.
For now I go, my precious one, to die
Among the legions of my noble Prince.
My dearest maiden, pray to God above
That I return alive from whence I go,
And happiness will come to you, my love,
For I shall take you as my wedded wife.'

And then those three great noblemen passed on.
'Tis them I seek upon this battlefield."

But Pavle Orlovich replied to her:
"O sister dear, O maid of Kosovo!
You see, my child, those lances, made for war –
How long they are, how solid, and how strong!
Such lances caused the blood of valiant men
To flow in torrents, and in floods so deep
That they would surge up to the stirrups of
A battle-horse, and to a warrior's waist!
All three of those you seek lie here in death.
Go home, my dear – go to your peaceful home;
Let not your skirt and sleeves be stained with blood!"

And when the maiden heard what he had said,
Her eyes gushed tears – they flowed upon her face.

– 70 –

THE MAIDEN OF KOSOVO

She sought her quiet home, and as she went
She wept, and palely uttered this lament:
"Oh bitter grief, how evil is my fate!
Should I embrace a young and green pine tree
It, too, would wither in its prime, and die."

8
The Death of the Mother of the Yugovichi

Dear God be praised, what wondrous happenings!
Amongst the Serbian host at Kosovo
There were the Yugovichi, brothers nine;
Old Yug-Bogdan, their father,[1] was the tenth.
The mother of the brothers Yugovich
Prayed God to grant to her a falcon's eyes,
And grant to her the white wings of a swan,
That she might fly above the battlefield
To seek her sons, nine brothers Yugovich,
And seek her husband, noble Yug-Bogdan.

   And God was pleased to hearken to her prayer.
He granted her a falcon's piercing eyes,
He granted her the white wings of a swan.
To Kosovo's broad level plain she flew.
She found her sons, nine brothers Yugovich,
All slain. And Yug-Bogdan lay with them, dead.
   Nine tall battle-lances stood above them,
Nine grey falcons stood upon the lances,
Nine great battle-horses tethered to them,
Nine ferocious hounds beside them standing.
   The battle-horses clamorously neighed,
The savage hounds beside them bayed aloud,
The dark grey falcons shrieked in wild outcry.
But in her breast the mother's heart was stone:
Her grief too deep to let the tears flow.

   She led the battle-horses from the field,
She brought away the nine ferocious hounds,
She took away the nine grey falcons too,
And went back, with them, to her quiet home.
   Her daughters-in-law saw her from afar;

As she drew near they met her on the road.
And now nine widows wept in wild lament,
Nine orphaned children cried in bitter grief,
Nine battle horses clamorously neighed,
Nine savage hounds together bayed and howled,
Nine dark grey falcons shrieked in wild outcry.
But in her breast the mother's heart was stone:
Her grief too deep to let the tears flow.

And when that night was at its darkest hour
Zelenko, Damian's horse, cried out aloud.
The mother asked the wife of Damian:
"O dearest daughter, wife of Damian,
Wherefore does Damian's Zelenko cry out?
It may be that he hungers for some wheat,
Or thirsts for water from the Zvechan's stream."
But Damian's wife in sorrow answered her:
"He does not hunger for a feed of wheat,
Nor does he thirst for water from the stream;
But Damian used to visit him by night
And, as a treat, give him some oats to eat,
And after midnight take him for a ride.
He cries in grief and loneliness for that
His lord and master comes to him no more."

And when the morrow's morn brought forth the day
There came two ravens flying, dark as night.
The wings of both of them were soaked in blood,
And both their beaks were lathered with white foam.
They bore a severed hand, a young man's hand,
And on one finger was a golden ring.
They threw the hand onto the mother's lap.

The mother took the hand and looked at it,
She dandled it, and turned it to and fro,
And then she called the wife of Damian:
"O dearest daughter, wife of Damian!

I pray you, say, whose severed hand is this?"
Her daughter-in-law, Damian's wife, replied;
"O dearest mother of my Damian,
That is the hand of Damian, your son.
O mother dear, I know it by the ring –
He wore that ring upon our wedding-day."

The mother took her son's hand in her own;
She dandled it: she turned it to and fro.
And then she whispered to the lifeless thing:
"How like an apple, O most precious hand,
That blossomed, came to fruit, and was cut down:
You grew up at my knee, but you were reaped
Upon the level plain of Kosovo."

Now, in her breast, the mother's heart was stilled.
No longer could she live to bear the loss
Of her nine sons, the brothers Yugovich,
And of her husband, noble Yug-Bogdan.

BALLADS OF
MARKO KRALYEVICH

9

Marko's First Heroic Deed

Among the hills rode Marko Kralyevich.[1]
His father rode beside him as he went
And, as they rode together, Marko laughed.
King Vukashin heard Marko laugh, and asked:
 "O Marko Kralyevich, my dearest son,
What is it that has caused you so to laugh?
Is it because I'm old and full of years?
Or is your joy in that fine dappled horse,
Or in the sword that hangs beside your flank?"
And gladly Marko Kralyevich replied:
 "My father dear, I tell you, in God's truth,
I do not laugh for any of those things –
Not for this fine strong dappled horse of mine,
Nor for the sword that hangs beside my flank,
And not because you're old, my father dear!
I thought of how, when I was but sixteen,
And this fine horse, my Sharats,[2] was but three,
I went one day to have him newly shod.
I had new horseshoes, ready for the smith,
I carried them in Sharats' saddlebag.

And, as I passed across this very plain,
There came from Yedren in the eastern lands[3]
A Pasha, and with him were sixty Turks,
And thirty maidens whom they had enslaved.
Their hands were tied, their arms were bound with ropes.
And when those captive maidens saw me there
Together, with one voice, they all cried out:
'O Marko Kralyevich! Brother in God!
Deliver us from these accursed bonds –
If not for gold, then out of chivalry –

For you will gain the love and blessings of
All thirty of us, and henceforth we shall
All serve you as we would a brother born!'

My father, I was saddened by their plight.
I went before the Turkish Pasha and
I bowed most deeply, to the very earth.
I kissed his hand, and kissed his garment too,
And then began, in humble tones, to speak:
'My noble lord, great Pasha of Yedren!
I beg you, set these thirty maidens free.
See! – I will pay you seven bags of gold!'

The Turkish Pasha heard: he turned his head
And glared at me for my temerity.
He took his whip: three leather thongs it had,
Then raised his hand and struck me with that whip.
He struck me many times; I could not count –
So hard he struck! But, when the shock had passed
I sought a weapon, father. I looked round,
But nothing could I see. But then I seized
The saddlebag with Sharats' shoes inside,
And that I swung. I struck the Pasha's head
A mighty blow – he fell dead on the grass.
And then I set about the other Turks.

Dear God be thanked, from whom all blessings flow!
Oh, what a sight it was, and what a din,
As I pursued those Turks around the field! –
The crashing horseshoes in my saddlebag!
The howling of the frantic, fleeing Turks!
The shrieks and cries of those poor captive girls!
Until, at last, was nothing living there,
Save for the maidens, whom I straight untied;
And them I sent their thirty separate ways
To tell of what had been, and what was done.

No more than that was passing through my mind –
Of how I beat the Turks, and did the deed
Without a bludgeon, and without a sword,
Or any knightly weapon in my hand.
And that is why I laughed, my father dear!"

10
Marko drinks Wine during Ramadan

The Sultan Suleman decreed these laws:[1]
"No man shall drink wine during Ramadan."[2]
"No man shall wear a coat that's coloured green."
"No man shall bear a sword of tempered steel."
"No man shall take a Turkish maid to dance."
    Marko[3] danced with all the Turkish maidens.
Marko bore a finely-tempered sabre.
Marko wore a coat of bright green colour.
Marko drank much wine during Ramadan –
And even forced the pious Muslim priests
And saintly hadjis[4] too, to drink with him!
    The Turks, outraged, brought word to Suleman:
"Mighty Sultan! Father and our Mother!
Did you not decree these stern commandments:
'No man shall drink wine during Ramadan.'
'No man shall wear a coat that's coloured green.'
'No man shall bear a sword of tempered steel.'
'No man shall take a Turkish maid to dance.'
– Marko dances with the Turkish maidens.
Marko bears a finely-tempered sabre.
Marko wears a coat of bright green colour.
Marko drinks much wine during Ramadan –
Nor does he only drink wine secretly,
But even forces pious Muslim priests
And saintly hadjis too, to drink with him."
    When Sultan Suleman heard this report
He called two messengers. To them he said:
"Go now, my trusty messengers, and say
To Marko Kralyevich that I, Sultan
Suleman, summon Marko to my Court!"

The two young messengers set off, and went
To Marko Kralyevich. When they arrived
Marko was drinking wine inside his tent;
Before him was a jug, five-gallon size.
The messengers were insolent, they brayed:
"Now pay attention, Marko Kralyevich!
The Sultan summons you before his Court!
So get you thence! Dally at your peril!"

   A furious rage seized Marko Kralyevich.
He took the jug that he was drinking from,
(Five-gallon size it was, and full of wine)
And smashed it on the Turkish messengers.
It broke their heads, and blood flowed with the wine!

   Then Marko went up to the Sultan's Court
And sat down by the Sultan, knee to knee.
He tipped his fur hat down upon his brow;
He drew his heavy bludgeon by his side,
And rattled his sharp sabre in its sheath.

   The Sultan Suleman then said to him:
"O Marko Kralyevich, my son, you know
Full well the orders that I have decreed:
'No man shall drink wine during Ramadan.'
'No man shall wear a coat that's coloured green.'
'No man shall bear a sword of tempered steel.'
'No man shall take a Turkish maid to dance.'
Now certain honest men speak ill of you.
They say you flout my every ordinance –
They say you dance with all the Turkish girls,
And that you bear a finely-tempered sword,
And that you always wear a bright green coat,
And that, in Ramadan, you drink much wine,
And even that you force our pious priests,
And saintly hadjis too, to drink with you.

   My son, why have you pulled your fur hat down?

Why do you draw that heavy bludgeon close?
And wherefore do you fidget with that sword?"

   Then boldly Marko Kralyevich replied:
"O my dear Father, Sultan Suleman!
If I drink wine in Ramadan, my Faith
Allows me: I am not a Mussulman.
And if I urge your priests, and hadjis too,
To drink with me, that is because I hate
Such sober fellows staring while I drink –
If they don't like it, let them stay away!
And if I wear a green coat, that's because
I am a young man and it suits me well.
And if I bear a finely-tempered sword,
It is my own, with honest money bought.
And if I like to dance with Turkish girls –
I am not married. O Sultan! – you too
Were once a young man, free of cares and wives!
And if I pull my cap down, that's because
It makes my face hot, talking to a king.

   And as for why I keep this mace in hand,
And why I make my sword free in its sheath –
I fear that there might be some argument!
If anyone should start a quarrel, though,
It would go hard for him who's nearest me!"

   The Sultan looked all round. No one
Was sitting nearer Marko than himself.
The Sultan edged away – Marko came too,
Until the Sultan was against the wall.
The Sultan searched his pockets then, in haste,
And found a hundred ducats, which he gave
To Marko: "There now, Marko, my good friend,
Take these, and drink as much wine as you want!"

11
The Ploughing of Marko Kralyevich

At home did Marko Kralyevich[1] drink wine,
Yevrosima,[2] his mother, drank with him.
And when they both had drunk their fill of wine
His mother sighed, and said to him: "My son!
I pray you, stop this fighting that you do,
For out of evil, sure, no good will come.
Besides, your poor old mother's getting tired –
Forever washing out your bloodied clothes.
Instead, go, take some oxen and a plough,
And turn the soil upon the plains and hills.
Then sow, my son, the seeds of golden wheat
That shall give nourishment to you and me."

Marko Kralyevich obeyed his mother.
He took a yoke of oxen and a plough,
But did not take his team to turn the soil –
Instead, he ploughed the Turkish highway up!
There came a troop of janissaries,[3] with
Three wagon-loads of gold, along the road.
"Marko!" they cried, "Stop ploughing up our roads!"
Cried Marko: "Turks! Stop trampling on my fields!"
Again: "Marko! Stop ploughing up our roads!"
And Marko: "Turks! Stop trampling on my fields!"

Then Marko, wearying of argument,
Took up both team and plough and slew the Turks
And, seizing all the treasure that they bore,
He took it to Yevrosima and said:
"O mother! See what I ploughed up today!"

12

How Marko went Hunting with the Turks

The Turkish Vezir Murat went to hunt
Among the green and pleasant hills, with twelve
Young Turkish huntsmen, in a band. There was
A thirteenth also – Marko Kralyevich.[1]
For three long days they hunted in the hills.
No quarry did they find in all that time.
At last they were rewarded in their quest;
They found a mountain lake, upon which swam
A plenitude of ducks with golden wings.

The Vezir launched his hawk to seize a duck,
But she would not be caught: she flew away
And soared up to the clouds, high in the sky.
The disappointed hawk came down to rest
Upon the branches of a green fir tree.
When Marko Kralyevich saw this, he said:
"Is it permitted, O Vezir Murat,
That I now fly my falcon, so that it
May take one of those golden-winged ducks?"
The Vezir Murat answered with good grace:
"Of course it is allowed, Marko, why not?"

So Marko launched his falcon into flight:
It soared up to the very clouds above.
It seized a gold-winged duck and flew
Down to the ground beneath a green fir tree.

Now, when the Vezir's hawk saw this it screeched
In jealousy and spite. Then, thinking it
Could steal the duck that Marko's falcon held,
It swooped down to it, raging, and it tried
To force the other to release its prey.
But Marko's falcon was as obstinate

And headstrong as its master – it fought back!
Tenaciously it held on to its prize.
In fury it drove off the Vezir's hawk,
And tore a bunch of feathers from its back.

But when the Turkish Vezir Murat saw
These happenings, he flew into a rage.
He picked up Marko's falcon in his hand
And dashed it savagely against a tree –
And broke its wing. Then, mounting on his horse,
He galloped off across the verdant hills,
The twelve young Turkish huntsmen following.

Now Marko's wounded hawk was hissing like
A nest of angry serpents in the rocks.
So Marko Kralyevich picked up the bird,
And carefully he bound its broken wing.
Then, angrily, he cried: "No good has come
Of this for you or me, my precious hawk!
To hunt with heathen Turks, without my friends –
Without my Serbian kin – I have done wrong!"

When Marko'd bandaged up his falcon's wing
He mounted Sharats and, in furious charge,
He spurred away into the darkling hills.
So like a mountain spirit Sharats flew,
So like a whirlwind, to the highest crest.
Then far below, upon the plain, they saw
The Vezir Murat, with his twelve young men.

And, looking up, Murat saw Marko there,
High in the mountains. To his men he cried:
"My children, O my twelve young huntsmen bold!
Do you see there, upon the mountain-top,
A swirling cloud? Inside that misty cloud
Is Marko Kralyevich. He rides Sharats.
May God help us – so furious they are!
No good will come … "

MARKO'S HUNTING

    Marko fell upon them!
He drew his shining sabre from its sheath
And, raging, charged towards Vezir Murat.
He chased the Turkish huntsmen round the field,
As harriers chase small birds among the thorns.
He reached Murat, and cut his red head off.
He reached the rest and chopped them all in half:
And so twelve huntsmen now were twenty-four!

    Then Marko stopped, and stood awhile in thought.
Should he now go to Yedren,[2] to the King,
Or should he go to Prilip, to his home?
He came to his decision, and he said:
" 'Tis better that to Yedren I should go
And tell the King of what has happened here,
Before some Turk denounces me to him."

So Marko went to Yedren, and there walked
Into the council-chamber of the King.
His face was dark with anger and with rage,
His eyes were flashing like a hungry wolf's:
As lightning in the mountains was his glance.

    And when the Turkish King saw him he said:
"Marko Kralyevich, my dearest godson!
Why so angry? Where are your good spirits?
Have you had bad luck, and lost your money?"

    Then Marko told the King of what had been,
Of what had happened, and what he had done.
And when the King had heard the tale, he laughed:
"Bé aferim![3] Well done, Marko, my son!
What's done is done. Had you done otherwise
I would no longer wish to call you son!
For any Turk can rise to Vezir's rank –
No man can equal Marko Kralyevich!"

    He dipped into his silken purse, and drew
A thousand golden ducats out of it.

He gave them all to Marko, and he said:
"Marko, my very dearest son, take these,
And go and get yourself some wine to drink!"
So Marko took the thousand golden coins,
And left the council-chamber of the King.

'Twas not for Marko's wine the King had paid.
No! – he had paid to make him go away,
For Marko's anger was so terrible!

13
...vich and Musa the Highwayman

Within a humble tavern in Stambol[1]
Sat Musa Arbanasa, drinking wine.
He drank his fill and, tipsily, he growled:
"It's now a good nine years that I have served
The Sultan, here in Stambol – and for what?
I have not earned enough to buy a horse,
A sword, or even an embroidered cloak,
Nor new nor second-hand. It isn't fair!
I've had enough! I'm off! I swear by God
I'll go down to the coast, and block the roads
That run along the sea – the ferries, too.
I'll build a fort of stone beside the sea,
With iron hooks upon its walls, and hang
A crop of priests on them, and pilgrims too!"

What Musa said in drink he, sober, did.
He left Stambol, went to the coast, and blocked
The ferries, and the roads beside the sea,
Along which all the Sultan's treasure passed.
There were three hundred wagon-loads a year,
And Musa stopped them all and stole the gold.
He built a fort of stone beside the sea,
With iron hooks upon the walls and gates,
And hanged upon them many travellers –
Both saintly hadjis,[2] and poor pilgrims too.

Now when the Sultan heard of Musa's crimes,
He sent against him Vezir Chuprilich
With under him three thousand men-at-arms.
But when they came upon him, by the coast,
Musa the Highwayman defeated them,
And killed them all. The Vezir, Chuprilich,

– 89 –

He took alive. He bound his hands, and tied
His feet beneath his battle-horse, and so
Despatched him to the Sultan in Stambol.

The Sultan then recruited mercenaries.
A boundless prize he promised to whomso
Should swiftly put an end to Musa's life.
But every one of them who tried his luck
Was quickly slain, and saw Stambol no more.

The Sultan now was overcome with rage.
Then Chuprilich the Vezir softly said:
"My lord, O mighty Sultan of Stambol!
The man for this is Marko Kralyevich[3] -
He'd put an end to Musa's banditry."

The Sultan looked at Chuprilich askance,
And tears came to his eyes; he wept, and said:
"O Chuprilich, this is but foolishness!
Why speak the name of Marko Kralyevich?
There's nothing left of him but rotting bones.
For you well know that, three long years ago,
I had him thrown in gaol. The gate was shut,
And never has that gate been opened since."

But Chuprilich said slily: "O Sultan!
What would you give, in charity, let's say,
To him who brought you Marko Kralyevich
Alive?" The Sultan cried: "To him I'd grant
The governorship of Bosnia, to have
And hold for nine full years, all free of tax!"

Then Vezir Chuprilich, on nimble feet,
Betook himself to Marko's prison gate.
He turned the key; he brought him out, and led
Before the Sultan – Marko Kralyevich!

His hair hung down, all matted, to the ground.
One half hung down; he clutched the other half
In front of him, to hide his nakedness.

MARKO AND MUSA

His nails, all overgrown, could serve as ploughs,
The foetid dungeon-stench had made him weak,
His face was blackened to the hue of slate.

The Sultan said to Marko Kralyevich:
"Are you, then, Marko? – are you still alive?"
"I am," said Marko, "But not at my best!"
The Sultan then told Marko all about
The wicked deeds that Musa had performed,
And all the harm he'd done. And then he said:
"Marko, can I have confidence in you?
Can I rely on you to go down to the coast
And there seek out and kill this highwayman?
I'll give you gold, as much as you may ask!"

But Marko Kralyevich said: "No, alas,
O Sultan! – that I cannot do. The stench
Of your foul dungeon's killing me. My eyes
Can hardly see. Like this, how could I join
In battle with Musa the Highwayman?
But put me in a comfortable inn,
Give me good wine, and give me rakia,[4]
And meat a-plenty from a good fat ram.
And fresh-baked loaves of good white wheaten bread.
Then, when some days have passed, I'll let you know
If I am fit and ready for the task."

The Sultan sent for three young hairdressers.
One washed Marko, another shaved his face;
The third one cut his hair and clipped his nails.
Marko was lodged, then, in a pleasant inn.
They brought him good red wine and rakia,
And meat a-plenty from a good fat ram,
And good white bread, as much as he desired.
There Marko stayed until, by slow degrees
His strength returned. He stayed there three full months!

The Sultan then asked Marko Kralyevich:
"Are you yet ready, Marko? Every day
I grieve to hear the sufferings of those
Whom Musa still oppresses without cease."

But Marko said to him: "Bring me a piece
Of cornel-wood that is completely dry,
From rafters of a roof that's stood nine years.
I'll see, then, if my strength has yet returned."

They brought to him a piece of cornel-wood,
And Marko tried to crush it with his hand.
Once, twice, and then a third time did he try,
But not a drop of moisture came from it.
"It is not time, O Sultan," Marko said.

So Marko stayed there for another month,
Until he felt his strength return still more,
And felt himself more ready for the task.
Again he called for pieces of dry wood;
Again they brought a piece of cornel-wood,
Again he crushed it in his strong right hand.
He crushed it twice, and then crushed it again –
And out of it two drops of water sprang!
And then at last did Marko Kralyevich
Say to the Sultan: "I am ready now!"

Then Marko went to see Novak the smith.
"Novak!" said Marko, "Make a sword for me –
The very best that you have ever made."
He gave him thirty ducats in advance,
And then went to a tavern, where he stayed
A full three days, and drank his fill of wine.
Then back he went to Novak, at his forge.
Said he: "Well, Novak, have you made my sword?"

Novak the smith brought him a bright new sword.
And Marko said to him: "Swordsmith Novak,
Is this a good sword? Answer truthfully!"

MARKO AND MUSA

Novak the swordsmith answered quietly:
"Here is your sword. My anvil's over there –
Now you can test it any way you please."

Then Marko took the sword in his right hand.
He raised it high and, with one mighty blow
Struck Novak's anvil, splitting it in two!

Then Marko said: "Smith Novak! Do you swear
That you have never forged a better sword?"
But then Novak the swordsmith said to him:
"O Marko Kralyevich, I will not lie.
Yes, I have made a better sword than this;
A better swordsman got a better sword.
When Musa left to go down to the coast
I made a sword for him, a special sword,
And when he struck my anvil with that sword
He shivered it completely, into dust!"

Now Marko Kralyevich was full of rage.
He said to swordsmith Novak, angrily:
"Hold out your hand, Novak, and take your fee!
Now shall I pay you for this sword you've made!"

Novak was gullible: the viper's sting
Of greed possessed him. He held out his hand,
And as he held it out, the sword blade flashed –
And Marko chopped his arm off with one blow.
He cried: "Novak, there's your reward! No more
Will you be forging swords, better or worse!
I'll pay a hundred ducats for this one
To see your lifetime out – what's left of it."

He gave Novak the money. After that
He saddled Sharats[5] and he rode away
Down to the coast, and looked for Musa there,
Asking for news of him from passers-by.

And, as the morn brought forth the day, upon
The harsh and craggy hills of Kachanik,
He came upon Musa the Highwayman,
Sitting upon his horse, at ease, legs crossed,
And idly throwing up his heavy mace
High in the air, and catching it again.

Marko approached. He stopped his horse and cried:
"Bold Musa, you are standing in my way!
Either you yield, or you must bow to me!"
But Musa Arbanasa said to him:
"Softly, Marko! Be not so quarrelsome!
Come, let's dismount, and drink a jug of wine!
I'll never yield to you, for you were born
Upon a feather mattress, in a room
Upstairs, upon the soft bed of a queen,
And swaddled in clean clothes of finest silk
With threads of gold; and softly you were raised –
On honey sweet and sugar you were fed.
But I was born in bleak Albania –
Delivered on the stone-cold rocks, among
The sheep, and wrapped in coarse black hessian,
In brambles cradled, and on gruel weaned.
My mother raised me hard, abjuring me
To stand aside for no man, all my life!"

When Marko of Prilep heard that, he hurled
His heavy spear, over his horse's head,
And straight it flew at Musa's manly heart.
But Musa parried it; he swung his mace
And turned the spear aside – it fell to earth.
Then Musa hurled his spear at Marko's breast:
But Marko met it squarely with his mace,
And shattered it in three parts, as it flew.

They drew their shining swords, of tempered steel,
And each attacked the other furiously.

MARKO AND MUSA

When Marko swung his sword at Musa's head
Bold Musa raised his mace and parried it,
And smashed the sword of Marko in three parts.
Then Musa struck at Marko with his sword,
But Marko caught the blow upon his mace
And snapped off Musa's sword-blade at the hilt.

They took their spiked bludgeons in their hands
And struck each other, blow for blow, with them.
So furiously they fought, they broke the spikes
And, seeing that, they threw them to the ground.

Then each dismounted from his battle-horse.
They seized each other's arms, and then began
To grapple, man-to-man, upon the field.
Those two great warriors were an even match –
Hero Musa equalled hero Marko;
Musa could not bring Marko to his knees,
Nor yet could Marko bring the other down.

And so those mighty heroes fought till noon
Upon that summer's day, both drenched in sweat –
Musa's lathered white, Marko's tinged with blood.
Then Musa shouted: "Marko, strike! – or I
Shall strike you down!" Marko struck out – in vain.
His blow was parried; it had no effect.
But Musa then struck Marko such a blow
That Marko fell upon the grassy field,
And Musa straddled him and pressed him down.
In anguish then did Marko Kralyevich
Cry out: "My guardian angel![6] Where are you?
I need you now – why are you not with me?
Have you betrayed me? Were your promises
To help me in distress worth nothing, then?"

And from the clouds above a voice was heard,
A mountain-spirit's voice, mysterious:

"How so, my brother, Marko Kralyevich?
Did I not always tell thee, wretched one,
That on the Sabbath thou shouldst never fight!
And shame 'twould be for two to fight with one.
– Forgettest thou the snake that, secret, strikes ..."

Now Musa turned his head to search the clouds
And hilltops whence the spirit voice had come,
And Marko drew a dagger that was hid
Within a secret scabbard in his clothes.
He thrust the knife deep into Musa's side
And ripped him open from waistband to throat!
So heavily did Musa's body fall
On Marko that he struggled to stand up.

And when Marko stood up and looked, he saw
That Musa had three hearts beneath his ribs –
Three hearts, together, in his manly breast.
One heart was stopped, the second beating still,
And on the third a deadly serpent slept.
The serpent woke and, as it raised its head,
So Musa's body jerked upon the ground.
The serpent, coiled on Musa's heart, then spoke:
"O Marko Kralyevich, give thanks to God
That I did not awake while Musa lived:
Thy travail, then, were worse three hundred-fold!"

When Marko Kralyevich saw this, he wept
And bitter tears flowed down upon his face.
"Dear God!" he cried, "Have mercy on my soul!
For I have slain a better man than me!"

He cut off Musa's head and put it in
His horse's nosebag. Mounting then, he rode
Back to the shining city of Stambol.

He threw the head of Musa down before
The Sultan's feet – who started up in dread.

Said Marko: "My lord Sultan, do not fear!
Think how you would have welcomed him alive,
When you do flinch to see his face in death!"

   The Sultan gave him three great sacks of gold.
Marko returned to Prilep, that fair town.
Musa remained alone at Kachanik.

14
Marko Kralyevich and the Eagle

Beside the road lay Marko Kralyevich,[1]
His body covered by his green dolman,
A silver-threaded shawl upon his face.
Beside his head his battle-lance was staked;
His horse, Sharats, was tethered to the lance.
And on the lance a golden eagle stood
And shaded Marko with its outspread wings.
The eagle brought cool water in its beak
And let the wounded Marko drink of it.

A spirit of the hills[2] in wonder cried:
"O golden eagle, tell me, in God's name,
Why do you succour Marko Kralyevich?
What bond of friendship do you have with him,
That you do spread your wings to give him shade,
And bring cool water to him in your beak?
What is this wounded human, then, to you?"

The eagle raised its noble head and said:
"Be silent, noisy spirit, hold your tongue!
I am beholden to this wounded prince
Who succoured me when I was in dire need.
Do you not know, or call to memory
How, when the armies clashed at Kosovo,
And in the battle both the kings were killed
– The Sultan Murat and Lazar the Prince –
Blood flowed in floods so deeply that it reached
The horses' stirrups and the warriors' waists,
And through it ploughed the raging hosts of men,
Horse crashed on horse, and man on warring man?
We hungry birds flew overhead in flocks;
We hungered all, and thirsted, as we flew.

– 98 –

But then we feasted on the flesh of men,
And drank the blood of men to slake our thirst.
My wings became all soaked in warriors' blood.
The sun was blazing in the cloudless sky;
The blood became encrusted on my wings
And hardened them: I could no longer fly.

The other birds took flight, but I could not.
I stood awaiting death upon the field,
Amid the trampling horses, and the men.
But God brought Marko Kralyevich to me:
He took me from the blood-drenched battlefield,
He took me to the peaceful woods so green,
And put me in a fir-tree, on a branch.

And when the teeming rain fell from the clouds
It washed away the blood, and cleaned my wings,
And I could spread my wings again, and fly
And soar above the green-clad mountain-tops,
And be at one again with my own kind.

I am beholden, for another boon,
To Marko Kralyevich, this noble prince.
Do you not know, or call to memory,
That when a town in Kosovo caught fire
Adjaga's tower burnt most fiercely?
Atop that tower my young eaglets lay,
Still flightless. It was Marko Kralyevich
Who rescued them, and wrapped them in a cloth.
He took them gently to his palace fair,
And there he fed them for a month of days
– A month of days, and then another week –
Before he brought them to the greenwood hills
And gave my little eaglets back to me.
These are the things that Marko did for me."

The memory of Marko Kralyevich
Is like a bright day in a sombre year.

– 99 –

15

How the Turks came to Marko's Slava

From year to year did Marko Kralyevich[1]
Pray God to grant that on Saint George's Day
– Saint George, his household's holy Patron Saint –
He might his Slava[2] celebrate in peace,
And that no Turk should desecrate the Day.

So, on the Holy Day of good Saint George
Did Marko call all people, high and low,
To celebrate his Slava, as was meet.
There were three tables set in his great hall:
At the first a dozen saintly bishops,
At the second all the Christian nobles,
At the third all poor and needy people.
To all the bishops Marko served the wine,
And all the Christian noblemen as well;
His mother served the poor and needy folk,
And Yelena[3] brought food for everyone.
Outside, Vaistina stood sentinel
To warn them if the heathen Turk should come.

There came three Agas of the Turkish King,
With thirty janissaries in their train.
All swaggering, they went to Marko's hall
And bawled at Vaistina: "Infidel!
Open the doors, you fool, and let us see
What happens here, on Marko's Slava Day!"

In Turkish tongue Vaistina replied:
"Have done! Let me alone, you Turkish lords!
The doors are shut. I fear my master's wrath:
And so I cannot open them to you."

The Turks took no account of what he said:
The janissaries all drew out their clubs,

And with their thirty clubs they smashed the doors,
Then, with those clubs, they beat Vaistina –
With six and thirty blows they battered him.
They beat his shoulders, and they bruised him sore.

But he, heroic, withstood, till at last
Could bear no more and fled into the hall
And went to Marko, weeping bitterly.

When Marko Kralyevich saw him, he said:
"Vaistina, my dear and faithful friend!
What is it, son? What mean these flowing tears?
Has hunger struck? Or do you thirst, my son?
If hunger ails you, here is food to eat;
If thirst, then here's cool wine for you to drink.
Now, stem your tears! Weep not, Vaistina!
Do not let not sorrow mar my Slava Day!"

The servant would not be consoled; he said:
"My noble master, Marko Kralyevich!
I do not weep for hunger or for thirst.
Misfortune is the bread that I must eat,
And evil is the wine that I must drink
In this, your noble and ancestral hall!
You sent me for a sentinel, a guard –
But did I do my duty as I should?

Three Agas of the Turkish King have come,
With thirty janissaries in their train.
These heathens came and shouted: 'Infidel!
Open these doors, you fool, and let us see
What happens here, on Marko's Slava Day.'

I answered softly, in the Turkish tongue:
'Have done! Let me alone, you Turkish lords!
The doors are shut. I fear my master's wrath:
And so I cannot open them to you.'

Those heathens did not heed what I had said.
The janissaries all drew out their clubs

And with their heavy clubs they smashed the doors,
And then they turned their heavy clubs on me
And beat my shoulders six and thirty times."

When Marko heard Vaistina's sad tale
He seized his massive bludgeon, and his sword,
And thus addressed the people: "Hear me, all
You gentlemen and nobles! I do swear
Upon the name of her who gave me birth
– Upon the Queen my mother's honoured name –
I can not decorate Prilep for you
With basil sweet or roses red, but yet
I'll garnish it with rows of Turkish heads!"

But then did Marko's mother plead with him
– His mother, that most honourable Queen:
"Forbear, I beg you, Marko, my dear son!"
Her breast she bared: "Consider, O my son!
Do not dishonour that which nourished you!
Forget not what a blessed day this is:
Upon your Day of Slava spill no blood!
But rather, whosoever comes to you
Give food to those who hunger, wine who thirst,
In honour of your sainted ancestors,
For your salvation and for Yelitsa's!"

Marko obeyed his mother's words. He put
Aside his sword, but held his bludgeon still.
With heavy heart he bade the Turks come in
And sit at table, all among the guests.
"Vaistina!" he said, "Bring wine for them!
Yela, my dear, bring food for them to eat!"
The servant brought them wine and rakia,
And Yelitsa served dainty food to them.

The Turks made merry as they swilled the wine.
When they had gorged themselves enough, they said
In heathen tongue: "Come, men, let's on our way,

Now we have seen and tasted all there is!"
(The Turks thought Marko did not understand,
But Marko'd sojourned in the Sultan's halls
In Sham of Turkey, far across the sea –
Lived there and served the Sultan seven years.
In all those years he learned their tongue as well
As if he had been Turkish born and bred).

And Marko now said to the Turks: "Sit down!
Stay seated! Drink more wine! And you must pay
The cost of physic for my servant's wounds!
Or, if it be that you decline to pay –
Stand up! – and I'll strike down the lot of you
One at a time, each with a single blow!
Know you my bludgeon? There is none like it,
For it is made of cold iron, forty okes,[4]
Of purest shining silver, twenty okes,
Of melted gold it has six okes as well.
So, six and sixty okes my bludgeon weighs!
You must agree that you deserve these blows,
Since you came here and battered down my doors,
And beat my servant six and thirty times,
And sorely bruised him with your heavy clubs!"

The Turks were seized with fear, and shivered all
To think of Marko's bludgeon, and its weight.
They pulled out twenty ducats, each of them;
The Agas pulled out thirty ducats each,
And put them in the pocket of his coat.
They hoped that this would end their misery:
They hoped that he would harry them no more.
But Marko would not leave the Turks in peace.
He now was full of drink and, drinking still,
Became more quarrelsome and menacing:
"Come, Turks, drink wine!" said Marko, "And it's time
For you to pay the customary tip!

My Lady Yela is no slave – she got
Her silken garments dirty, serving you!"

   Confusion struck the Turks. In haste they sought
What money they still had, and pulled it out,
And those that had none borrowed from the rest.
Ten ducats each was all that they could find
The Agas twenty. Marko took the lot
And put it in his pocket with the rest.

   Then Marko went back singing to the hall.
"Yevrosima, my mother dear!" he said,
"I have not robbed the Turks of all this cash;
I'd never take what is not owed to me –
They gave me all of it most willingly!
Now let bards sing! Let now the tale be told
Of how Turks fare who wish to deal with me!"

   The Turks, all wailing, left the hall in tears
And, speaking Turkish to each other, cried:
"May God forbid that any one of us
Should ever, after this, go visiting
An infidel upon his Slava Day!
The price we've paid today for one small meal
Would be enough to feed us for a year!"

16

The Death of Marko Kralyevich

One Sunday Marko Kralyevich[1] arose
   At dawn, before the day's great heat had come,
Below the sea-girt heights of Urvina.

   As Marko rode upon the mountain-side
There came a wondrous happening; his horse,
Sharats, began to falter and to weep.
The like of this had Marko never seen
And, troubled in his mind, he gently said:
"What ails you, Sharats? What is it, my friend?
For eight score years have you and I been one,
And never have you stumbled heretofore.
Yet now, today, you falter, and you weep –
You stumble, and the tears run down your face.
God be with us! No good can this forebode.
A mortal life is coming to its end –
Perchance it is my life, perchance 'tis yours."

   As Marko said these words, a voice rang out
From Urvina's high wind-swept mountain-tops –
A spirit voice,[2] mysterious, which said:
"Marko Kralyevich, my friend and brother!
Know'st thou not why Sharats weeps and falters?
He laments the end of thee, his master:
Thou and he shall very soon be parted."
   But Marko cried: "Pale spirit, hold your tongue!
And may your throat grow sore! How could it be
That from my Sharats I should ever part?
For we have passed through cities and through lands,
And travelled all the world from east to west,
And never have I found a finer steed
Than Sharats, or a braver man than me?

I will not be parted from my Sharats
While my head remains upon my shoulders!"

But from the mountain-tops the voice replied:
"Marko Kralyevich, my dearest brother,
No man ever can take Sharats from thee;
Nor canst thou be done to death by any
Deed of man, or blow of any weapon –
Be it battleaxe, or lance, or sabre –
No man living in this world can slay thee.
But death shall come, O Marko, by the hand
Of God, the ancient executioner.

If thou believest not, hear what I say:
When thou hast ridden to the mountain-top
Look well about thee, both to left and right.
And thou shalt see two slender fir-trees there,
Which stand up higher than the mountain's peak,
All shimmering and bright, with leaves of green.
Between them is a well of water, pure
And clean. To that place shalt thou ride Sharats,
And there dismount. Tie Sharats to a tree.
Go to the well: look on the water's face.
And there upon its surface, calm and clear,
Thou shalt see thine own image, and thy Death."

Marko obeyed the mountain-spirit's words.
He rode up to the very mountain-top,
And looked about to left and right, and saw
There were two slender fir-trees, side by side,
Which stood up higher than the mountain's peak,
All shimmering and bright, with leaves of green.
And Marko rode on Sharats to the trees.
Dismounting there, he tied Sharats to one.
The well was there, its surface clear and calm,
And when he looked upon the water's face
There his own image and his Death he saw.

MARKO'S DEATH

The tears flowed down on Marko's cheek. He cried:
"O faithless World! Life was a bright flower
That bloomed so beautifully a little while –
A very little while – three hundred years.
The time has come that I must pass away."

Then Marko Kralyevich put forth his hand,
And from its scabbard drew his shining sword.
He went to Sharats, his beloved horse,
And with one heavy blow cut off his head,
So that no Turk should ever ride Sharats,
Or force him into menial servitude,
Or load his back with copper water-casks.

And when Marko had slain his horse, Sharats,
He buried him. A better grave he made
For Sharats than his brother Andria.[3]

His shining sword he snapped in pieces four,
So that it would not fall in Turkish hands,
So that no Turk could ever boast that he
Possessed the sword of Marko Kralyevich,
And so that Christendom should not be shamed.

His sword destroyed, Marko then broke his lance
In seven pieces, and he threw them up
Into the branches of the slim fir-tree.

Then in his strong right hand Marko took up
His mighty bludgeon, armed with many spikes
And, from the very heights of Urvina,
He hurled it down into the azure sea.
Cried Marko: "When it rises from the sea
A hero such as I will be reborn!"

With all his weapons gone, he put his hand
Inside his belt, and took from it a pen,
And clean white paper from his pocket took.
Then on the paper Marko wrote these words:

"O you, who come to Urvina to find

The well of water here, between the trees,
And here see Marko lying as in sleep –
Know you, that Marko Kralyevich is dead.
There are three bags of treasure on my belt.
What sort of treasure? – golden ducats all.
The first I give, with all my blessings, to
Whoever undertakes my burial.
The second to the Church I do bequeath.
The third is for the lame, and for the blind;
That they may all walk forth into the world
And sing of Marko, and his memory!"

   When he had finished writing, Marko took
The paper, and he put it in the tree,
So that it could be seen by passers-by.
His golden pen he threw into the well.

   Then Marko Kralyevich took off his coat –
His green dolman – and laid it on the grass
Beneath the trees. He crossed himself and lay
Down on his coat, his cap upon his face.
He then was still. He did not rise again.

   Day after day he lay, beside the well.
He moved not. Marko Kralyevich was dead.
And people, passing on the broad highway,
Would see him lying there – asleep, they thought.
They kept away, for fear of waking him.

   Where fortune is, there is misfortune too;
And in misfortune, fortune can be found.

   And fortunate it was that on that road
Came Vasa, saintly Abbot of the church
Of Vilindar,[3] on Athos' holy mount,
And with him his disciple, Isaia.
When Vasa saw Marko, he put his hand
Upon Isaia's right arm, and he said:
"My son, be quiet, lest you waken him!

MARKO'S DEATH

For Marko's always surly when he wakes;
If we disturb him we could come to harm."

The Abbot noticed how still Marko lay,
Then saw the paper in the tree above.
He went and took it down, and studied it,
And read that Marko Kralyevich was dead.
He got down from his horse and, still unsure,
The Abbot Vasa gently shook Marko –
But Marko had been dead for many days.

The tears flowed down on Abbot Vasa's cheek,
For Marko's death was bitter grief to him.
He took the bags of gold from Marko's belt,
Unbuckled them, and fixed them to his own.

But then he stood in thought, with troubled mind;
Dead Marko's body called for burial.
Long pondered he – then inspiration came.
He lifted Marko's body, and put it
Upon his horse, then rode down to the sea.
He seated Marko on a galley's bench,
And sat beside him as they crossed the sea.

The galley sailed to Athos' holy Mount,[4]
And there the Abbot took Marko ashore.
He took him to the church of Vilindar.
There, in the church, the proper services
And funeral hymns were sung for Marko's soul.
Then, near the church, was Marko laid to rest.

There was no headstone raised, or any mark,
So that the grave might nevermore be found;
So that no enemy might ravage it.

BALLADS OF
THE OUTLAWS

17
How Miyat Tomich became an Outlaw

Thanks be to God from whom all blessings flow!
How beautiful is Duvno's level plain![1]
There flourishes the wheat in golden fields,
And on its grassy meadows horses graze.
But all this loveliness is overcast
With misery. The Turkish overlords
Have seized the land and made it their domain.
And Miyat Tomich[2] has been dispossessed.

   The Kadi of Zhupanyats, Suzitsa,[3]
Was now the master and, at harvest-time
Two hundred men were made to reap the crops,
Among them Miyat Tomich, once their lord.
A Turkish overseer drove them on.

   The reapers gathered at the break of day.
They took their scythes and sharpened them with stones,
Then spread out side-by-side to reap the wheat.
All were surprised that Miyat was not there.
A little time had passed – it was not long –
When Miyat Tomich came upon the field.
He wished them all "Good morning!" pleasantly.
In kind they answered, and they smiled at him.

   Murat, the overseer, did not smile.
Instead, he drew his sabre from its sheath
And snarled at Miyat Tomich: "Hey! You there!
You good-for-nothing unwashed infidel!
I'll teach you to mock your Turkish betters!"

   He swung his sword to cut off Miyat's head,
But Miyat nimbly dodged the Turk's attack;
He sprang aside, and drew a loaded gun.
He fired the pistol, and his aim was true –
His bullet hit Murat straight through the heart.

The Turk fell down – no pillow for his head,
And where he fell he stayed, for he was dead.
   Then Miyat Tomich shouted to the men:
"Stop! Reap no more! You know these fields are mine –
My patrimony, and so dear to me!
But now, so long as I remain alive,
We'll see who dares to stay and harvest them.
Let any man of courage follow me –
I'll be his haiduk-captain,[4] none so bold!"
And into Vran's high mountains[5] Miyat went.

   There went with him a goodly company.
The men of Duvno joined him willingly.
They counted it no ill to die in war.
Overcoats, for them, were home and shelter,
Pistols were their brothers and their sisters,
Muskets were their mothers and their fathers,
And not a man among them feared the Turk.
   And oft by night they came to Zhupanyats,
And there they plundered and they robbed the Turks –
Much booty took, in gold and precious things
(And bribes to stay away, in good hard cash).
Enraged, the Turkish gentry howled aloud,
And cursed Kadi Suzitsa bitterly
Because he could not stop Miyat Tomich,
Or save them from his dreaded company.

When Suzitsa the Kadi heard of this
He ordered heralds through the land to go,
And publicly announce, from dawn to dusk:
"Among you is there not a mother's son
Who's brave enough to climb the hills of Vran
And find this poisonous serpent in his lair,
And capture him, or else bring back his head?
The Kadi surely will reward him well –
The fields of Miyat Tomich are the prize,

And with them Miyat's sister, as a slave,
The Kadi's daughter, Fata, as a bride –
A dowry of three hundred ducats, too!"

In Zhupanyats young Turks abounded, who
Thought highly of themselves, and of their arms.
All bragged that they would catch Miyat Tomich.
So loud their boasts, they came to Miyat's ears,
In his high fastness in the hills of Vran.

There Miyat sat, within a rocky cave,
His company around him, drinking wine.
When Miyat leisurely had drunk his fill,
With ruddy cheeks, he called out to his men:
"My brothers, drink until the sun has set!
Tonight there'll be for us a hunter's moon
To light us on our way to Zhupanyats.
It's time we called upon that fine Kadi
And paid our grazing-fees – they're overdue!"

Among the haiduks there was no dissent.
They all prepared. They tied their bootstraps tight,
Their haversacks they buckled on their backs,
Their slim Italian muskets shouldered they,
And heavy clubs they carried in their hands.

So, after nightfall, when the moon was up,
To Zhupanyats came Miyat with his band.
The time was chosen well – the dead of night,
Long after evening prayers, when everyone
Was sound asleep. Then Miyat knocked upon
The courtyard gate of Suzitsa's fine house.
A sleepy servant called out from within:
"Who's there? Who knocks at this ungodly hour?
Good men should be in their soft beds, asleep!"
The haiduk-captain, Miyat Tomich, said:
"I'm from Kongora village. I'm the son
Of Kongora's Chief Elder, and I want

To wed a fair young maiden: we're betrothed.
Her mother's willing, but her father's not,
And to another lad he's promised her.
I've brought her here – I've brought my wedding-guests.
We've come to see the Kadi, Suzitsa.
I'll give the good effendi three gold coins,
Five rams entire, and five good gelded ones,
If he will marry us, right here and now!"

    The servant told the Kadi what was said.
Suzitsa's eyes grew big and round with greed,
And he himself went to the courtyard gate.
He opened it – and let the haiduks in!

    And now Miyat confronted Suzitsa;
In rage and bitter anger Miyat cried:
"You Turkish hog! Monster of gluttony!
You've forced us all to live in poverty!
You've driven me to live with mountain wolves –
Now you go and join your saint, Muhamed!"

    His sword flashed – he struck off Suzitsa's head.
He searched his house, and plundered all his goods.
He found his sister, Marian's mother, there,
And freed her from her hateful slavery.
The Kadi's daughter, Fata, did he seize.
But he disdained to harm the Kadi's wife –
He left her, so that she could kneel beside
His grave and pray for his immortal soul.

    Then, taking Fata, Miyat Tomich left
And led his company to Christian lands.
His haiduks then became his wedding-guests.
The Kadi's lovely daughter was baptised;
So Fata's name to Katya now was changed,
And she became his loving wedded wife.
On Miyat's wedding-day they all rejoiced
And all gave praise and thanks to mighty God.

Fair Katya stayed at home beside the sea,[6]
While Miyat ranged the mountains far and wide.
He seized much treasure: many Turks he slew.
Much wealth he sent to Katya, so that she
Might dress becomingly, and tend his house.
So, when he visited his sea-girt home
He found abundance there, of beast and fowl,
And good white bread, and handsome silken clothes.

O friends and brothers! all of this is true.
The spirits of the mountains tell the tale.
No mother ever bore a son so bold,
No company of haiduks has there been
To equal that of Tomich Mihovil!
So many Turks he slaughtered, that his arms
Were drenched up to the elbows in their blood.
To infants in their cradles he brought fear,
As widows made he many women grieve,
And sisters cry for brothers they had lost.

18

Starina Novak and Bold Radivoye

Starina Novak[1] sat and drank red wine
Upon the green slopes of Romania.[2]
With him his brother Radivoyé[3] sat,
The lad Gruyitsa sat with them as well,
Beside Gruyitsa sat young Tatomir,
And thirty haiduks more, all in a band.

And when the haiduks all had drunk their fill,
And when the wine had mellowed all their minds,
Upon a sudden, Radivoye cried:
"Hear what I say, O Novak, brother mine!
I'm going to leave you now; the time has come.
The years lie heavy on you – you're too old
For banditry, and living hard, and war!
No longer shall you lie in wait with me
For fine fat merchants travelling the roads!"

And when bold Radivoye said these words,
Straightway he leapt up to his feet, and took
His slim Italian musket in his hand.
The thirty haiduks leapt up too, and went
With him, away, across the darkling hills.
But Novak stayed, beside a green fir tree,
And with him stayed the two young boys, his sons.

But see bold Radivoye's cruel fate!
He chanced upon a crossing of the ways
Where great misfortune came to him, for there
Upon the road was Mehmed Arapin,
A mighty Turk, with three great sacks of gold,
And thirty men-at-arms escorting him.
The Turk saw Radivoye and his band.
Immediately he called his men-at-arms

SERBIAN EPIC BALLADS

Who, quick as light, drew sword and fell upon
The thirty haiduks, who did not have time
To raise their muskets. Every one they slew,
And, having slain them, cut off all their heads
But Radivoye's – him they took alive.

   They bound his hands with ropes, and led him off
Along the highway through the craggy hills.
They mocked him as they went, and bade him sing.
So Radivoye raised his voice and sang:
"God's curse upon you, high Romania!
Among your summits is there not a hawk?
For see! – a flock of doves is passing through,
And leading them there is a dusky crow.
They take along with them a pure white swan;
They carry treasure underneath their wings!"

   As thus sang Radivoye on the road
The boy, Gruyitsa, heard the song he sang,
And straightway went to Starina Novak:
"O father, listen! On the highway there
A man is singing as he passes by.
He sings of high Romania, and of
The fierce hawk that dwells among the heights.
For sure it's uncle Radivoye's voice!
Perchance he comes with treasure in his hands,
Or else misfortune has befallen him.
O father, hurry! We must go to him!"

   Gruyitsa took a musket in his hand,
And went to set an ambush on the road.
Beside him went his brother Tatomir,
And old Starina Novak followed them.
But when they came upon the broad highway
He chose the spot; all three in hiding lay.

   And now the sound of hooves rang round the hills,
And on the road the thirty Turks appeared.

And each Turk on his shoulder had a lance,
And on each lance was stuck a haiduk's head.
In front of them rode Mehmed Arapin,
And he led Radivoye, tightly bound,
And carrying the three great sacks of gold.
Beneath the hills they went along the road
Until they came to where the ambush lay.

   Starina Novak chose the moment, and
He shouted to his two companions.
He fired his musket, and his aim was good,
For Novak's shot hit Mehmed Arapin –
The bullet pierced his waist and stopped his breath,
And he was dead before he fell to earth.
The Turk had fallen on the grassy verge,
And Novak leapt out from his hiding-place,
And struck Arapin's head off with his sword.
He then cut Radivoye free, and put
The Turk's own sword in Radivoye's hand.

   Thanks be to God, from whom all blessings flow!
They fell upon the Turks and scattered them.
They drove them to each other, round and round –
So those who fled from Radivoye's sword
Were run through by the sword of Tatomir,
And those whom Tatomir pursued
Were spitted on the sword of Gruyitsa,
And any who escaped from Gruyitsa
Were soon despatched by Starina Novak.
They killed them all, and cut off all their heads.
And then they seized the treasure of the Turks,
Those three great sacks of gold – a worthy prize –
And sat down by the road to drink red wine.

   When they had drunk, Starina Novak said:
"Well, Radivoye, headstrong brother mine!
What say you now? Give me your answer true!

Which were the better – thirty bold young men,
Or old Starina Novak, full of years?"

And Radivoye answered him at once:
"Starina Novak, O dear brother mine!
Far better were my thirty lusty friends –
But then, they did not have an old man's luck!"

It may go hard for him, however bold,
Who will not heed the prudence of the old.

19

Starina Novak and Knez Bogosav

Novak[1] and Radivoye[2] drank their wine
Upon the icy River Bosna's bank.[3]
Knez Bogosav[4] was in their company.
Said Bogosav, when they had drunk their fill:
"Come now, Starina Novak, my old friend,
Speak straight – give me your answer truthfully!
What made you join the haiduks?[5] Why was it?
What dread misfortune drove you to this pass –
To risk your neck, to live hard in the hills,
To follow the harsh trade of banditry,
In your old age, with little time to live?"

Starina Novak answered: "My good friend
Knez Bogosav, I tell you, truthfully,
It was indeed a hard and bitter thing.
There was a time – you will remember it –
When Smederevo town was fortified.[6]
The Turk Yerina set the work in hand.
I was conscripted and was forced to work.

For three long years I laboured with no pay.
Day after day I shifted wood and stone;
I used my cart and oxen for the work.
In those three years of labour I received
No recompense in cash, and none in kind.
I did not earn a pair of sandals' price!
I'd pardon her for strengthening the fort
Of Smederevo, but she went beyond –
The walls were massive, and the towers high.
The gates were gilded, and the windows too.
For this they placed a tax upon the land.
The rate for every house, three pounds of gold
– My brother, that's three hundred ducats each! –

– 121 –

All those who had the money paid the tax
And, having paid it, they were left alone.
But I was just a poor man, with no means.
I could not pay – I did not have such wealth.

   I took my working pickaxe and I fled
Into the mountains, where the haiduks are.
In my home town I could no longer stay
And suffer under that damned Yerina.
Instead, I journeyed to the Drina's shore,[7]
And thence to where the rock-bound Bosna flows.

   And, as I went through high Romania,[8]
A Turkish wedding-party came in view.
They led the bride, a lady of high birth.
Without a care they passed along the road,
But one young Turk, the bridegroom, lagged behind,
And he was riding on a fine bay horse.
That man was not content to pass in peace.
Instead, he lifted up his heavy goad –
A three-pronged goad it was, with copper horns –
And with it thrashed my shoulders, savagely!

   Three times I begged him, in the name of God:
'Good bridegroom, stop! Do not do this to me!
Today you have good fortune, pride, and strength:
This is your day of happiness and joy!
Leave me alone: go on your way in peace,
For I am but a poor man, as you see!'

   In vain – the Turk would not leave me alone,
But went on beating me, more furiously!
He bruised me sorely, and I was in pain.
Then raging anger overcame my mind –
I took my pickaxe from my shoulder and
Struck upwards with it, at him, on his horse.
I struck not hard, but yet I toppled him;
He fell down from his horse upon the ground.

NOVAK AND BOGOSAV

At once I ran to him. Two or three times
I struck him with my pickaxe, and at that
The spirit left his body, and he died.

   I then went through the pockets of his coat.
I found three bags of money in them, which
I took, and put away inside my shirt.
I took his heavy sabre from his belt
And buckled it on mine. Then, by his head,
I stuck my pickaxe in the stony ground
So that the Turks could dig a grave for him.
   I mounted, after that, the Turk's bay horse
And made my way to high Romania.
The Turkish wedding-guests had seen all this.
It seems they did not wish to follow me –
Perhaps they did not wish, or did not dare.

   In these last forty years I have become
Accustomed to Romania's rugged heights.
I love them better than my own birthplace.
For here I guard the roads between the hills.
The Sarayevo[9] merchants I waylay
And take from them their silver and their gold,
Their precious silks, and velvet cloth, so I
And all my company can dress like kings!
   For I am skilled in sally and retreat,
And I can deal with perils of all kinds –
There is no one I fear but God Himself."

20
Old Vuyadin

The maiden called a curse upon her eyes:
"O my dark eyes, I would that you were blind!
You looked, and yet today you did not see
The Turks of Liyevno[1] as they passed by,
Leading in chains three haiduks[2] from the hills –
Old Vuyadin and his two gallant sons."

   All three were dressed magnificently, like lords.
Old Vuyadin wore on his back a robe
Of scarlet cloth, all trimmed with fur and gold,
Like those the Pashas wear to sit in State,
And Vuyadin's son Milich wore the same.
His brother Vulich wore upon his head
A fur hat with twelve feathers in a ring,
Each feather made of gold, a pound in weight.

   And when they came in sight of Liyevno,
Of that accursed city, Liyevno,
Its great white tower shining in the sun,
Old Vuyadin spoke sternly to his sons:
"My sons! You pair of falcons! Do you see
Before us Liyevno, that cursèd town -
Its great white tower shining in the sun?
There they will beat us, and will torture us.
There they will break our bones, our arms, our legs,
And tear our staring eyes out from our heads.
My sons! Each one a falcon! Do not show
That in your breast there beats a coward's heart,
But show them how a Serbian hero dies!
   Do not betray our countrymen, not one!
Do not betray our helpers, those good folk
Who let us share their homes in winter-time,

And safely hide away our hard-won gold.
Do not betray the keepers of those inns
Who welcome us, and give us wine to drink,
And let us drink our wine in secrecy."

And when they came at last to Liyevno
The prison gates were shut behind them all.
Three days they waited, while the Turks conferred
On how they could inflict the greatest pain.

And when those three long days had passed away
They took old Vuyadin and broke his bones.
They broke his arms, they broke his legs, and as
They started to gouge out his eyes, they said:
"Speak, Vuyadin, you dog, and tell the truth!
Tell us, you cur, where all the others are –
Where are the rest of your accursed band?
Tell us who your collaborators are,
Who let you share their homes in winter-time,
And safely hide away your stolen gold.
Tell us, you dog, who those innkeepers are
Who welcome you, and give you wine to drink,
And let you drink your wine in secrecy!"

But old Vuyadin answered with these words:
"You talk in jest, you stupid Turkish fools!
I did not speak to save my sturdy legs
Which never failed, though horsemen hunted me!
I did not speak to save my two strong arms,
Which let me break a warrior's lance in two,
And let me fend a naked sabre-stroke!
I will not speak to save my lying eyes,
Which led me into dread misfortune here,
Which looked down from the highest mountain-tops,
Which looked down on the highways far below,
Where pass the Turks and merchants, to and fro ... "

21
Mali Radoyitsa

God save us all! What dreadful sound is this –
Like thunder, or the quaking of the earth?
Do storm-waves crash upon a marble shore?
Are mountain-spirits locked in warlike strife?
It is not thunder or the quaking earth,
Nor do the stormy seas beat on the shore.
'Tis not the roar of spirits waging war.
No! – Turkish guns are being fired for joy!
The Aga Bechir-aga feasts in glee,
For Mali Radoyitsa[1] has been caught
And cast into the dungeon far below.

   Within the dungeon twenty captives lay,
And all of them were wailing grievously.
But one sang out, and tried to comfort them:
"Dear brothers mine, be not so filled with fear!
For God will not forsake us: He will send
A hero who will surely rescue us!"

   But when Radé was thrown into their cell
They all with one accord cried out and wept,
And in their misery they cursed him so:
"God damn you, Rade! We are all dead men!
In you was all our trust, that surely you
Would some day get us out of this foul gaol.
Now look at you – a prisoner like us!
What hero is there left to set us free?"

   But Mali Radoyitsa answered them:
"Do not be so afraid, dear brothers all!
Hear what I say! – as soon as morning comes
Call Aga Bechir-aga urgently:
Tell him that Mali Radoyitsa's dead
And that his body calls for burial."

So, when the sun had risen in the east,
The twenty captives all called out aloud:
"O Aga Bechir-aga, God damn you
For putting Radoyitsa in with us!
You should have hanged the fellow yesterday!
Instead, he died amongst us in the night –
Must we all perish from the pestilence?"
   The dungeon doors were opened, and they brought
Poor Mali Radoyitsa's body out.
Then Aga Bechir-aga ordered them:
"You prisoners! Take him, and bury him!"

   But his wife, Bechir-aginitsa, spoke:
"Wait! Look again! This Rade is not dead –
Not dead at all, but shamming like a fox.
Bring fire and burn his feet! We'll see if that
Will make him move, and show he lives – the dog!"
They lit a fire on Rade's feet, but he
Possessed a lion's heart – a hero's soul,
And not a movement or a murmur made.

   But then said Bechir-aginitsa: "Hah!
Well, fancy that! But Rade is not dead –
Not dead at all, but shamming like a fox.
Now bring a snake, a deadly serpent here,
And put it on his breast that it may strike!
The filthy cur will flinch or stir at that!"
They brought a deadly serpent, and they thrust
Its savage mouth on Rade's breast, but he
Possessed a lion's heart – a hero's soul,
And not a movement made, nor did he flinch.

   Again said Bechir-aginitsa: "Hah!
Well, fancy that! But Rade is not dead –
Not dead, but still he's shamming like a fox.
Drive twenty spikes beneath his nails! We'll see
If that will bring this rotten scum to life!"

SERBIAN EPIC BALLADS

They then brought twenty spikes and hammered them
Beneath all Rade's toe and finger nails.
But even this did not break Rade's heart –
He made no movement in his agony.

And now said Bechir-aginitsa: "Hah!
How strange this is! But Rade is not dead.
I know he lives, but's shamming like a fox.
The girls must dance before him! Haikuna,
The loveliest of all, shall lead the dance.
He surely will be moved to smile at her!"

The dancing-girls assembled, joining hands,
And beautiful Haikuna stood with them.
She led them up to Rade as they danced,
With supple swaying limbs, in front of him
– May God destroy her, vile deceiving witch! –
She was the tallest and the loveliest,
Her elegance and grace outshone them all,
Her beauty gave enchantment to the dance.
The soft silk trousers rustled, and the sound
Of small soft-slippered feet seduced the sense.
And Rade glanced at her – his left eye looked,
His right cheek twitched, and recognition passed.
But when the maiden Haikuna saw that,
She slipped the silken kerchief from her throat
And laid it on his face, to hide his eyes,
That no one else should see. "Father!" she cried,
"Let not this sinfulness go on. He's dead –
Let him be buried. Fetch the prisoners!"

But then said Bechir-aginitsa: "Lord!
This carrion's not fit for burial.
Take it, instead, and throw it in the sea –
The boundless sea – so may the fish rejoice
To feast on such fine, tender bandit-meat!"

MALI RADOYITSA

    The Aga took Rade far out to sea,
And threw him in, and left him there for dead.
But Rade was a swimmer! With strong strokes
He swam across the sea, until at last
He stood upon the shore, then shouted out:
"Come now, you fine white teeth of mine! Pull out
These dreadful spikes I have beneath my nails!"
Then Rade sat cross-legged on the ground
And, one by one, drew out the twenty spikes
And put them carefully inside his shirt.

    Still Rade would not stay or rest, but when
The night was fallen, and when all was dark,
He went to Aga Bechir-aga's hall,
And stood beside the window, listening.

    The Aga sat at supper in his hall,
His wife beside him, and he said to her:
"O noble lady! O, my dearest wife!
These last nine years, since Radoyitsa came
To rob and pillage, there has never been
A day when I've been free of fear of him,
Or any night when I could dine in peace.
All thanks to God that he is here no more,
And that I've put an end to him at last!
As for those twenty others – come the dawn
Tomorrow, and I'll hang the lot of them!"

    But Mali Radoyitsa saw and heard.
He sprang into the room – seized the Aga –
Dragged him from his very dining-table –
Grasped his jaw in one hand, and his shoulder
In the other – then he wrenched his head off!
And after that he seized the Aga's wife.
He took the twenty spikes out of his shirt
And started driving them beneath her nails.
But ten of them he'd hammered in, before

The shrieking bitch gave up the ghost and died.
And Mali Radoyitsa said to her:
"O Bechir-aginitsa, now you know –
Now you yourself have felt the agony!"

Then Rade turned to Haikuna, and said:
"Haikuna, my own heart's delight, find me
The dungeon's key, that I may now at once
Set free the twenty captives lying there."
Haikuna went and found the dungeon's key,
She brought it, and he set the captives free.
And then he said: "Haikuna, my sweet love,
Give me the keys of all the treasure-chests.
I need to have some money in my purse:
The journey to my home is very long,
And on the way I'll need to buy some wine!"
She opened then a box all full of gold.
But Rade said: "Haikuna, my dear heart,
What use are all these golden coins to me?
Should I make golden horseshoes out of them
To shoe my steed? – Alas, I have no horse!"
She opened next a chest of silver coins –
He shared them out among the prisoners.

And Rade then led Haikuna away.
He took her to his home in Serbia,
And to a white church there. Her Turkish name,
To Christian changed, became Andjelia,
And Rade took her as his loving wife.

BALLADS OF
THE NOBLEMEN

22

The Death of Voivoda Priyezda

So many letters came, and yet still more.
From whence came they, and whither did they go?
From Mehmed, king of all the Turks, they came
To Stalach town,[1] and to the Voivoda
Priyezda[2] there, and in this manner read:
"Priyezda, Voivoda of Stalach town!
Send me at once your three most precious things:
The first of these your finely-tempered sword,
That cuts through wood, and stone – aye, even iron;
The second, that fine horse that you call Zhdral,
That in one bound can overleap two walls;
The third, your own true love, Yela, your wife!"

When Voivoda Priyezda read these words
He sat to write, and this was his reply:
"O Mehmed, king and lord of all the Turks!
Draw up your army, strong as you may please;
To Stalach come, whenever you may please;
Besiege the town, in any way you please –
Of my possessions I'll not give you one!
My fine sharp sword I forged for my own hand,
And Zhdral, my horse, I nurtured for my own.
My dearest wife is mine, and mine alone –
And I'll not give you one of these, my joys!"

King Mehmed gathered up his army; then
To Stalach came, and laid siege to the town.
For three long years he beat against the walls,
But no breach made, nor yet a stone could budge,
Nor any way could find to conquer it –
Nor would he raise the siege and march away.

One morning early, on the Sabbath's eve,
Priyezda's wife stood on the battlements
Of Stalach town, and cast her gaze below,
Upon the River Morava beneath.
And Morava flowed troubled by the walls.
Priyezda's wife was anxious, and she said:
"Priyezda, O my master and dear lord!
I fear the Turk may dig a tunnel 'neath
The Morava, and so invade the town."
But Voivoda Priyezda said: "My love,
I beg you, hold your peace and have no fear –
No man could dig beneath the Morava!"

And then it was that fateful Sunday dawned,
And all the gentlemen together went
To church, and there they took Communion.
The Service ended, and they came outside,
And Voivoda Priyezda called to them:
"O gallant captains! You that are as wings –
My very wings – together we shall soar!
Come, let us dine and let us drink good wine,
Then let us fling the gates of Stalach wide
And throw ourselves once more upon the Turk –
And may God grant us good deliverance!"

And then Priyezda called his wife: "My dear!
Go down, I pray, into the cellar. Bring
Us rakia[3] and wine, that we may drink."

So Yela took two golden jugs, and went
Down far below, to where the cellar was.
But when she came before the cellar door
She found it full of Turkish men-at-arms!
She saw them drinking wine, their shoes as cups.
She heard them toast her health in ribald jest –
To Priyezda the toast was: "Rest in peace!"

When lady Yela saw this dreadful sight

She dropped the jugs: they clattered on the floor.
She ran back to her husband, in his hall:
"Woe is your wine, my precious lord!" she cried,
"Woe is your wine, and tears your rakia!
The cellar's full of Turkish men-at-arms!
They're drinking wine – cool wine – their shoes as cups.
They toast us both – they drink 'Good health!' to me,
But 'Rest in peace!' to your immortal soul –
While you still live, they drink upon your grave!"

Then Priyezda the Voivoda leapt up –
Flung wide the gates – they rushed upon the Turks,
And battle raged. And on that field there fell
Sixty Serbian lords, but of the heathen
Thousands perished.

                Then Priyezda came back
Inside the town, and shut the gates behind.
He drew his mighty battle-hardened sword,
And with it he struck off his horse's head.
"My Zhdral!" he cried, "My dear, most precious joy!
No Turkish king shall ride upon your back!"
And then he snapped that fine sharp sword in two:
"My precious sword!" he cried, "My good right arm!
No Turkish king shall hang you on his belt!"

And then Priyezda went in to his wife.
He took her hand, and said: "O Yelitsa,
My dearest lady, wise and faithful wife!
Is it your wish to perish, now, with me,
Or to become a chattel of the Turk?"

The tears flowed on Lady Yela's cheek:
"I wish to die, in honour, with you, now.
I will not love in shame the heathen Turk;
I will not cast aside the One True Faith,
Nor will I trample on the Holy Cross."

The two clasped hands and climbed up on the walls
Of Stalach town. Then Lady Yela said:
"Priyezda, dearest master and my lord!
The Morava has nourished us from birth –
The Morava shall take us now in death."
Together, then, they leaped into the flood.

The Turkish king Mehmed took Stalach town.
Of all the things he craved he took not one.
In rage he shrieked: "God damn you, Stalach Town!
I came here with three thousand men-at-arms,
But not five hundred do I lead away."

23

How the Brothers Yakshich shared their Inheritance

The Moon rebuked the Day-star angrily:
"Where have you been, you wayward star, and what
Have you been doing for the last three days? –
Just idling and wasting time, I trow!"
But quietly the Day-star answer made:
"Yes, I have been away. I stayed awhile
Above Belgrade's fair city, looking down,
And there I saw a wondrous happening.
I saw the Yakshich brothers,[1] Dimitar
And Bogdan, share their great inheritance."

   The brothers both agreed, in amity,
To share their patrimony equally.
Dimitar took the lands of Karavlah[2]
And Karabogdan,[3] and with them he took
The Banat,[4] to the River Danube's shore;
While Bogdan took the level land of Srem[5]
And all the plain beside the Sava's flood,
And he took Serbia, to Uzhitse.
To Dimitar fell lower Belgrade town
Where, by the Danube, stands Neboisha's tower,
While Bogdan took the upper town, where stands
The church of Ruzhitsa – 'twas all agreed.
The merest trifle separated them:
A little thing, not worthy of dispute –
Just one grey hawk and one black battle-horse.
Dimitar claimed that, as the elder son,
The horse and hawk should both belong to him,
But Bogdan would not give up either one.

SERBIAN EPIC BALLADS

The next day, at the very break of dawn,
Dimitar mounted on a fine black horse
And took a grey hawk on his wrist, but then,
Before he rode off to the hills to hunt,
He called his wife, Andjelia, and said:
"Andjelia, my good and faithful wife!
It is my wish that you do kill Bogdan
My brother – poison him! And if you fail
Then quit my house and nevermore return!"

And when she heard these awful words, his wife
Andjelia was wracked in misery.
She sat in thought, and to herself she said:
"What cowardice! – that he should order me
To kill his brother with a poisoned draught! –
A dreadful sin before the face of God,
And in mens' eyes a crime most horrible!
For people, great and lowly, all will say:
'See! Look at her! – that shameless wretch, who killed
The brother of her husband – poisoned him!'
But if I do not poison him, what then? -
I must for ever leave my hearth and home."

As thus she thought, a thought came to her mind.
She went down to the cellar of the house,
And there she took a holy chalice, wrought
Of finest gold, a chalice that had been
Her loving father's wedding-gift to her.
She filled the chalice with the choicest wine,
And took it her brother-in-law; then
She kissed his hand, she kissed his garment's hem,
And, bowing to the ground, she said to him:
"My honourable brother, take this gift –
This chalice and the wine and, in return,
I pray you, give the hawk and horse to me!"

Bogdan was chastened by the lady's words,
And gave the hawk and battle-horse to her.

Now Dimitar was hunting in the hills,
But nothing had he found the live-long day.
Towards the evening he chanced to come
Upon a mountain lake, with waters green,
And on it swam a duck with golden wings!
Dimitar cast the grey hawk into flight
To take golden-wingéd duck as prey.
But she would not be taken: she fought back.
She grappled with the hawk and, in the fray,
She broke the hawk's right wing and flew away.

When Dimitar Yakshich saw what was done,
He stripped his lordly clothing off in haste,
And plunged into the silent lake: he swam
To fetch the hawk and bring it to the shore.
And as he held the injured bird he said:
"My precious hawk, oh say! how is't with you
Without your good right wing to bear you up?"
In pain and grief the hawk replied to him:
"Without its wing a hawk is like a man
Whose brother is no longer by his side."

Dimitar then remembered that his wife,
At his command, would kill his brother born.
He leapt upon the great black battle-horse
And galloped like the wind to Belgrade town,
In hopes to find his brother still alive.

As he approached the wooden bridge he spurred
The great black horse to cross at breakneck speed.
The horse's pounding hooves crashed through the bridge –
Headlong it fell, and both its forelegs broke.
Now Dimitar was full of anxious fears.
He took the saddle off the horse's back:

He slung it on his shoulder, on his mace,
And ran into the town, towards his house.
As he approached, he shouted to his wife:
"Andjelia, my faithful wife! – oh, say
That you have not yet killed my brother born!"
 Andjelia his wife replied to him:
"I have not killed your brother, no! Instead,
I have made peace between the two of you."

24
Ailing Doichin

Doichin, that noble Voivoda,[1] fell ill
Within the city of Salonika.
Nine years he lay in pain upon his bed.
The people of the town had seen him not
In all that time, and thought that he was dead.
The news of this was carried far and wide –
So far abroad, it spread to Arab lands,
And to the ears of Uso Arapin.

Immediately he saddled his black horse
And came in strength upon Salonika.
When he arrived below Salonika
He laid siege to the town; his camp was spread
About the level plain without the walls.
He called upon the citizens to send
A champion to meet him on the field,
And fight in single combat, to the death.

There was no hero in Salonika
To meet his challenge, and to fight with him.
Doichin there was, but he was sick in bed.
Duka there was, but he had hurt his arm.
And Iliya was but a callow youth
Who never in his life had seen a fight,
Far less had ever taken part in one –
And even had he wished, he could not go
Because his aged mother thus forbad:
"You may not go, Iliya, foolish boy!
Black Arapin would best you in a fight,
And he would kill you, Iliya, my son,
And leave me childless in my latter days."

Black Arapin, when he was told of this,
And learned that in Salonika there was
No man prepared to meet him in the field,
Imposed a tax upon Salonika:
From every household there, a good fat ram,
From every hearth, a loaf of wheaten bread,
A barrelful of good red wine, besides
A jug of rakia – the finest sort –
And twenty yellow ducats in hard cash,
And one young maiden too, to go to him –
A maiden fair, whether betrothed or not.

The goods came in from all Salonika,
And all of them were brought to Doichin's hall.
But Doichin was not there to gather them.
His faithful wife was in the house; with her
There was his dearest sister, Yelitsa.
These ladies sadly gathered all the things
Together, but could not deliver them,
For Arapin would not accept the goods
Unless Yelitsa went to him herself!
The ladies both were overcome with grief.

Yelitsa sat beside her brother's bed
And wept; the tears ran down her pallid cheeks
And fell in drops upon her brother's face.
And Doichin, in his suffering, became
Aware of them and in confusion cried:
"My servants – may the Devil damn you black! –
You're drenching me with water – curse you all!
Will you not leave me here to die in peace?"

But Yelitsa, his sister, softly said:
"Poor Doichin! O dear ailing brother mine!
Your servants are not dampening your face –
These are your sister Yelitsa's own tears."

But Doichin, on his bed of pain, replied:
"For God's sake, sister, what are you about?

Are you complaining over lack of bread,
Or are you short of food, or good red wine?
Have you not gold enough, or linen cloth?
Or have you no embroidery to do,
Or do you lack the wherewithal to sew?"

But Yelitsa his sister answered him:
"Poor Doichin, O dear ailing brother mine!
I have abundance of good wheaten bread,
And plentiful amounts of good red wine.
I have enough of gold and linen cloth.
I have embroidery that I can do;
I have the wherewithal to weave and sew.
No, brother dear, our troubles are much worse –
For Uso Arapin has come in force.
He holds the field and has besieged the town.
He called on us to send a champion
To fight in single combat to the death.
There was no hero in Salonika
To meet his challenge, and to fight with him.
And when black-hearted Arapin knew this
He laid a tax upon Salonika:
From every household here, a good fat ram,
From every hearth, a loaf of wheaten bread,
A barrelful of good red wine, besides
A jug of rakia – the finest sort –
And one young maiden too, to go to him,
A maiden fair, whether betrothed or not.

From all Salonika the tribute came,
But when it was this household's turn to pay –
You have no brother here, to organize
The ordering and transport of the goods,
So we poor women did it all ourselves;
We put together all Uso's demands,
But we can not deliver them to him,
For Arapin refuses them, unless

AILING DOICHIN

I, Yelitsa, your sister, go to him.
Now hear me well, poor Doichin, brother mine!
I can not love this Uso Arapin,
As long – O brother, hear me – as you live."

Then Doichin, in his sickness, cried aloud:
"Salonika, oh may you burn in hell!
Why could you find no champion to fight
In single combat with this Arapin,
And leave me here alone, to die in peace?"

But then he called his wife, Andjelia:
"Andjelia, my true and faithful wife!
Is my bay horse, my Doro, still alive?"

Andjelia, his wife, replied to him:
"Doichin, my ailing husband, noble lord!
Your bay horse Doro lives, and he is fat,
For I have tended him and fed him well."

Then ailing Doichin spoke thus to his wife:
"Andjelia, my faithful loving wife!
Take Doro to the blacksmith's to be shod.
Petar the Blacksmith is my blood-brother.
Ask brother Petar, for true kinship's sake,
To give me credit, and to shoe my horse.
I shall, myself, fight Uso Arapin;
I have to go, whatever fate may bring."

She did what he had told her straightaway.
She took Doro, the great bay battle-horse,
And led him to Petar the Blacksmith's forge.
And when Petar the Blacksmith saw her there
He greeted her, and spoke with honeyed words:
"Andjelia, my brother's lovely wife!
Has my old blood-brother, then, died at last,
And have you brought his Doro here to sell?"

The beautiful Andjelia replied:
"My brother Petar, Doro's not for sale.

SERBIAN EPIC BALLADS

Doichin, your blood-brother, is still alive.
He asks you, for the kinship that you bear,
To give him credit, and to shoe his horse,
For he must fight with Uso Arapin.
When he returns he'll pay you for the shoes."

But blacksmith Petar only laughed, and said:
"Andjelia, my darling sister dear!
I want cash down before I'll shoe a horse.
But you may stay with me, and let me kiss
Your lovely eyes, until Doichin returns
And pays me for the shoeing of his horse!"

Andjelia began to curse and swear –
Enraged, she blazed up like a living flame.
She led Doro away, though still unshod,
And went back home to Doichin, in his hall.

When she returned, sick Doichin said to her:
"Andjelia, my faithful loving wife!
Did Petar shoe my Doro properly?"

But, hissing like an angry snake, she said:
"O suffering Doichin, O my noble lord!
May God destroy your blood-brother Petar!
He wants cash down before he'll shoe your horse,
Unless I stay with him until you pay.
He lusts for me, to kiss my very eyes!
But never will I love Petar the Smith
As long as you, Doichin, are still alive."

And when the ailing Doichin heard these words,
He said: "Andjelia, my loving wife!
Go now to Doro, my fine battle-horse,
And put his harness on, and saddle him,
And after that, bring me my battle-lance."

And then he called his sister, Yelitsa:
"O Yelitsa, my sister very dear!
I pray you, bring a roll of heavy cloth,

– 146 –

AILING DOICHIN

And bind my body tightly, from my thighs
Up to my neck, and round my chest and ribs,
To hold my aching bones together and
To stop them grating each upon the next."

They quickly went and did as they were bid.
His wife prepared Doro and saddled him,
And brought her husband's battle-lance to him.
His sister brought a roll of heavy cloth,
And tightly bound her brother's body up;
She bound him from his thighs up to his neck.
They clipped his German sword on to his belt.
They brought him Doro, his great battle-horse.
They helped him mount upon the horse's back,
And handed him his heavy battle-lance.
Now Doro sensed the battle soon to come –
He pranced and reared and snorted in his joy

And, as they clattered through the market-place,
So powerful his stride, his hooves dug up
The very cobblestones and scattered them!
The merchants of Salonika cried out:
"Now let us all give praise and thanks to God!
Not since the time that Doichin passed away
Have we seen such a hero riding through
Our shining city of Salonika,
Upon a battle-horse as fine as this!"

Then Doichin rode out on the level plain
Towards the camp of Uso Arapin.

And when black Arapin saw Doichin come
He leapt up to his feet in shock and fear.
He stayed inside his tent, and shouted out:
"Hey, Doichin, may God damn your soul to hell!
How can it be that you are still alive?
Well, come along, my friend, and let's drink wine –
The devil take our quarrel and our fight!

I'll lift the tax upon Salonika!"
    But ailing Doichin sternly answered him:
"Come out to me, black Arapin, you dog!
Come out, and on the field of honour stand!
You challenged me in battle: I am here!
No longer shall you laze, and drink red wine,
And fondle giggling girls inside your tent!"
    But Uso Arapin called out to him:
"Oh, come now, brother, Voivoda Doichin!
Be not so haughty and so quarrelsome!
Dismount, and join me – let us drink red wine!
I'll free Salonika from paying tax,
And let the city's maidens all go free.
And I do swear, before the One True God,
That I will go away, and not return."

    When ailing Doichin saw that Arapin
Was scared to fight, and would not leave his tent,
He spurred his great bay horse, and rode towards
The fine pavilion of his enemy.
He tore the canvas open with his lance –
And what a sight appeared before his eyes!
Inside the tent were thirty pretty girls,
And in the midst of them was Arapin.

    When Arapin saw Doichin would not bend,
And that he would not let him go in peace,
He mounted on his great black battle-horse.
He took his mighty battle-lance in hand
And rode out on the wide and level plain.
The battle-horses stamped in fierce joy!

    And ailing Doichin called to Arapin:
"Now strike, black Arapin, you filthy cur!
Strike first, you dog, and may your aim be bad!"
    Black Arapin then hurled his battle-lance
To pierce the aching body of Doichin.

AILING DOICHIN

But Doro was a wily battle-horse! –
He bent his legs and dropped down to the grass,
And Arapin's flung lance flew overhead.
It struck the stony ground behind and broke,
So half the lance was sticking in the earth,
The other half lay shattered by its side.

And when black Arapin saw all was lost
He turned his back and galloped, in full flight,
Towards the city of Salonika,
With Doichin following, across the plain.
As Arapin approached the city gate
Doichin was there behind him, on his heels.
Then Doichin flung his heavy battle-lance
And nailed Arapin to the city gate!

Then Doichin drew his shining German sword
And cut the head off Uso Arapin.
He spun the head upon his sharp sword's point,
And out of it he dug Arapin's eyes.
He wrapped the eyes up in a piece of cloth,
And threw the empty skull down on the grass.
Then Doichin rode back to the market-place.

When Doichin came beside the blacksmith's forge,
The forge of his blood-brother, smith Petar,
He shouted to the blacksmith, still inside:
"Come out, my brother! I am here to pay
The price I owe you for your blacksmith's work.
You gave me credit when you shod my horse."

But Petar stayed inside. He called to him:
"O my blood-brother Doichin, there's no need!
No payment's due – I never shod your horse.
I said I would not – that was just in jest,
My brother! – but Andjelia cursed and swore,
In rage, she blazed up like a living flame,
And took the horse away, though still unshod."

But ailing Doichin called to him again:
"Come out! I wish to pay the shoeing fee."

Then Petar came outside his blacksmith's forge,
And ailing Doichin raised his shining sword,
And with one blow he struck off Petar's head.
He spun the head upon his sharp sword's point,
And out of it he dug the blacksmith's eyes.
He wrapped the eyes up in a piece of cloth,
And threw the skull down on the cobblestones.

Then Doichin went back to his noble hall.
Dismounting there, he left Doro outside,
And went to lie upon a cushioned couch.
He then took out the eyes of Arapin
And threw them to his sister. "There!" he cried,
"My sister, take the eyes of Arapin!
Be sure, my sister dear, you will not kiss
Those eyes so long as I am still alive."
Then from the cloth he took the blacksmith's eyes
And gave them to his wife, Andjelia:
"Andjelia, these are the blacksmith's eyes.
Be sure, my loving wife, you will not kiss
Those eyes so long as I am still alive."

Those were his words. He spoke them, and he died.

25

The Ban of Zrin and the Maiden Begzada

For nine long years the noble Ban of Zrin[1]
Groaned in captivity; for Mustai-beg,
The Bey of Novi,[2] had imprisoned him.

One day most bitterly he cursed the Turk:
"God strike you down and damn you, my lord Bey!
I am the last of all your prisoners;
The rest you have set free, exchanging them
For great estates, or villages, or land,
And some you have released upon parole,
Or given them their freedom for much gold.
The gold I offer you, you will not take!"
Mustai-beg answered: "Noble Ban of Zrin!
You shall not ever leave this place again.
First Friday, our great Turkish feast, draws near.
On that day you shall be impaled, alive,
And then paraded through the army's ranks!"

When Mustai-beg had said these dreadful words
The Ban of Zrin said quietly to him:
"Then I must ask you, my lord Mustai-beg,
To let me have the wherewithal to write:
Some paper, pen, and ink, that I may write
A letter, which I can despatch to Zrin
In Krayina,[3] and to my mother there,
To tell her that she'll see me nevermore;
To ask for proper clothes to shroud my corpse –
Now that I am so soon to meet my death."

These words surprised the Bey. Nevertheless
He gave the Ban the wherewithal to write:
Some paper, and a pen, and pot of ink.
The Ban then wrote a letter, which he sent

To Zrin in Krayina. It did not tell
His aged mother to abandon hope
Of ever seeing him again. Instead,
This was the letter which he wrote to her:
"My most dear and venerable Mother!
Send to me my silver tamburitsa.
In its case there is a golden casket.
In the casket are two precious jewels –
Each of them is worth a city's ransom."

And when the Ban had finished writing it
The letter went, it passed from hand to hand,
Until it came to Zrin in Krayina,
And to his venerable mother there.
She took the letter and, when she had read
The words her son had written, she shed tears.
At once she wrote a letter in reply
And sent it to him, in his prison cell;
With it the silver tamburitsa went.

And when the Ban received the instrument
He sat and looked at it, and smoked his pipe –
He smoked his pipe and gently stroked the strings.
He drew from them a melody, and sang:
"My tamburitsa, friend of passing hours!
My aged mother, ever dear to me!
For you I do not grieve that I must die,
But that I never took a maid to wife,
Who could have loved you as a daughter should.
Alas! No daughter and no grandchild's there –
No daughter who could serve and comfort you,
Nor manly grandson your support to be
For all your life, until your dying day.
To whom shall pass my lands and villages?
To whom shall pass my treasures and my gold?
Who shall inherit my Banovina?"[4]

THE BAN OF ZRIN

The Ban had sung as if he were alone,
With none to overhear the song he sang.
But Begzada the maiden heard it all –
Begzada, lovely sister of the Bey –
For she stood by the window of his cell,
And she looked through the window, at the Ban.

The maiden wore a dress of cloth-of-gold,
With more gold strands than threads of pure white silk;
Her throat adorned with seven necklaces –
Two necklaces were of red coral beads,
Two necklaces were of black coral made,
Two necklaces were made of fine white pearls,
The seventh necklace was of golden coins,
– And that one was a necklace of three rows,
A hundred golden ducats in each row –
Which gleamed and gently tinkled as she moved.

Her eyes were black, and shone like sloe-berries.
Her arched eyebrows were like a seagull's wings.
Her eyelashes were as a peacock's plumes,
Shading her roseate cheeks. So sweet her lips
That when she spoke 'twas like a cooing dove,
And when she smiled, as though the sun had shone.

And when the Ban of Zrin had sung his song,
The maiden Begzada then spoke to him:
"O Ban of Zrin, tell me – is it the truth
That you have never married, have no wife?"
"It is the truth, fair Begzada," he said,
"My precious darling, you can trust my word:
The truth of what I say is firm as stone –
I am a nobleman, but have no wife!"

Then Begzada the maiden said to him:
"O Ban of Zrin, my dear, my precious love!
How say you – am I pleasing in your sight?
Will you not take me now to be your own,

And to become your loving wedded wife?"
The Ban cried out: "What foolishness is this?
How can I take you for my wedded wife,
When I am here, condemned, in this dark cell,
Imprisoned in your own dear brother's fort?
You know the Turkish feast, First Friday, comes.
Your brother's going to kill me on that day –
I'll be impaled alive upon a stake,
And then paraded through the army's ranks!"

But Begzada the maiden softly said:
"O Ban of Zrin, trust me! Abandon fear!
And pray to God that this dark night shall pass,
And make way for the morrow's shining day.
For then I shall obtain this prison's key –
I'll come to you, and I shall set you free.
And I shall make you ready, and send you
Upon the road to Zrin in Krayina,
And to your loving mother's open arms!"

And so the Ban of Zrin devoutly prayed
To God that that dark night should pass away.
The dark night passed, and bright day came again;
That long day passed, and then night fell once more.

And, when the night was at its darkest hour,
Came Begzada at midnight to the cell.
Three barbers were with her, and in her hand
She held the key that locked the prison door.
She then unlocked the door and opened it.
She took the Ban's hand, and she led him out
Away from there, and to a house nearby –
The barbers following upon her heels.

One shaved him while another trimmed his nails;
The third young barber cut his light brown hair
And, when the prison-filth was washed away,

THE BAN OF ZRIN

They saw upon him many wounds, that had
Been slow to heal, where snakes had bitten him.

And then the maiden led the Ban of Zrin
Into a room upon an upper floor.
It was her very brother's dressing-room
– Bey Mustai-beg of Novi's dressing-room!
And there she dressed him in her brother's clothes.
She put on him a finely woven shirt –
More golden threads than linen in the cloth;
A pair of trousers with glass buttons on –
A golden dollar fixed upon each one;
Between the buttons, heavy silver chains,
With golden yellow ducats fixed to them.
She dressed him in her brother's dolman then,
And there were eighteen buttons on that coat –
In two rows, nine a side, all down the front.
Each button spoke of wealth extravagant,
For every one was worth two okes of gold![5]
Another button was there, at the throat:
That button spoke of wealth superlative –
Three okes of gold that button would have cost!
That button had been made into a clasp.

– For when young men are drinking good red wine,
And find that many glasses make them hot,
They will undo the button at the neck
(That way the wine slips down more easily),
And when they've had enough, they do it up!

Upon his head she placed a Turkish cap,
Adorned with golden feathers, nine in all,
The ninth was curved round in a circle full,
And tapped against the other golden plumes.
She wound a jet-black turban round his head,
Such as the Turkish janissaries wear[6]
When visiting the waters of Djumai –

A hundred groschen was that turban worth!
The maiden wound the turban round the cap,
So that the golden plumes should make no sound.
She put about his waist a silken belt.
She slipped two pairs of pistols into it,
One pair short-barrelled, and the other long;
With them a broad knife, and a scimitar.
She clipped an ammunition belt on him,
Equipped and charged with sixty cartridges.
Fine silken socks she put upon his feet,
And leather shoes with narrow turned-up points.
She put on him a lordly riding-cloak,
So large it covered horse and rider, both,
And blazoned with embroidery of gold.

   When Begzada had fully dressed the Ban,
She went downstairs to where the stables were.
She chose the very best two horses: like
A swift was hers, and like a swallow his.

   The Ban was silent: nothing did he say.
And Begzada the maiden said to him:
"O Ban of Zrin, my own dear precious love!
Why are you silent? Won't you speak to me?
Am I no longer pleasing to your eyes?
Or is it that you have a wife at home?"
   The Ban of Zrin replied to Begzada:
"O Begzada, my own most precious love!
It is not that you do not please my eyes,
Nor is it that I have a wife at home.
My thoughts are overcast – I cannot see
How you and I may ever leave this town.
How shall we pass through Novi's city gates?
The gates are shut; Mumin the Gatekeeper,
With sixty watchmen under his command,
Is guarding them. This Mumin knows me well –

THE BAN OF ZRIN

That he will recognize me there's no doubt."

But Begzada the maiden said to him:
"O Ban of Zrin, this is but foolishness –
We shall with ease depart from Novi town:
There'll be no hindrance at the city gates.
As we approach them, draw your cloak above
Your head – conceal your face. Then, spur your horse
Most urgently – use spur and goad on him!
And that way we shall pass through Novi's gates."

So when they rode up to the city gates,
The maiden Begzada called out aloud:
"Hey, Mumin! Gatekeeper! Bestir yourself!
The Bey's in pain; he has nine hurting teeth.
He suffers so, he cannot hold his horse.
There is no time for chatter – open up!
The Bey must get to Sana's river, fast,
For there is rioting and trouble there!"

Mumin the Gatekeeper was ill at ease.
He wondered, but he did not dare to ask
Why no man rode as escort to the Bey,
Except the maiden Begzada herself.

So, through the gates of Novi town they passed
And, once they were outside the citadel,
They sped away across the level plain,
Like shooting stars that streak across the sky.

The Ban was silent; nothing did he say.
And Begzada the maiden said to him:
"O Ban of Zrin, my own dear precious love!
Why are you silent? Won't you speak to me?
Am I no longer pleasing to your eyes?
Or is it that you have a wife at home?"

The Ban of Zrin replied to Begzada:
"O Begzada, my own most precious love!
It is not that you do not please my eyes,

– 157 –

Nor is it that I have a wife at home.
Before us is the Sana, swift and cold –
That cursed river: there's no way across.
Uso the Bulyubasha[7] guards the bridge
With soldiers, and he knows me very well.
While I was in your noble brother's gaol
This Uso was my gaoler for three years,
And he will recognize me, there's no doubt."

But Begzada the maiden said to him:
"O Ban of Zrin, hush! Do not be afraid!
The Sana's crossing will not trouble us.
As we approach the Sana river's bridge
I'll pass to you a brightly-coloured scarf.
You wrap it round your head, then cover it
By pulling up the collar of your coat –
That coat that covers both you and your horse.
Then spur your horse, that is as swallow swift –
Drive him with spur and goad, and make him leap
Up high, as if to fly across the foam!
And we shall cross the Sana's icy flood!"

So, when they reached the River Sana's bank,
She gave the Ban a brightly-coloured scarf.
He wound it round his head, and covered it
By pulling up the collar of his coat –
That huge greatcoat that covered man and horse.
He spurred his horse, that was as swallow swift –
Drove him with spur and goad, and made him leap
Up high, as if to fly across the foam.

And as they reached the drawbridge, which was closed,
The maiden Begzada called out aloud:
"Hey! Bulyubasha Uso! Stir yourself!
The Bey's in pain: he has nine hurting teeth.
He suffers so, he cannot hold his horse.
Open the bridge! – no time for chattering –

THE BAN OF ZRIN

The Bey is riding to Hungarian lands!"

    Uso the Bulyubasha was not sure.
He wondered, but he did not dare to ask
Why no man rode as escort to the Bey,
Except the maiden Begzada herself.

    Then Begzada, impatient, raised her hand
In which she held a heavy Tartar whip.
With it she thrashed Uso; she broke his skin,
And where his skin was broken, dark blood flowed.
So she beat Uso: Uso beat the guards.
In haste they let the heavy drawbridge down –
The bridge that spanned the Sana's icy flood!

    Thanks be to God! It was a wondrous chance
That they had crossed the Sana just in time!
For barely had they crossed when, from Novi
The signal-guns were fired to spread the word
That Begzada, fair sister of the Bey,
Had been abducted, and with her had gone
Two horses of the Bey – the finest pair!
Too late! The Ban and Begzada rode on;
They sped away across the level plain,
Like shooting stars that streak across the sky.

    And still the Ban was silent; spoke no word.
And Begzada the maiden said to him:
"O Ban of Zrin, my own most precious love!
Why are you silent? Won't you speak to me?
Am I no longer pleasing to your eyes?
Or is it that you have a wife at home?"

    The Ban then answered: "Begzada, my dear!
In Novi, when I pledged my troth to you,
It was because I was in fear of death.
Now I must tell the truth. I have a wife
At home; I have two little sons as well."

When Begzada the maiden heard these words
She shrieked. Dear God! It was an awful thing
To hear the maiden keen in misery,
To hear her screams of deep and bitter grief,
To see her fling her body to and fro,
Just as a swallow darts, and turns, and twists!

The Ban consoled her gently, and he said:
"Fair maiden, do not weep: be not so sad.
I am not taking you to be a slave,
But rather am I making you a bride!
My nephew is another Ban, and he
Is taller, and is comelier than I,
And his domains are greater far than mine!"

When to the Ban's fair hall they came at last
The Ban's two sons ran out to greet their Sire.
They cried: "May God be with you, father dear!"
The Ban said: "My dear sons, God be with you!
Your grandmother, is she within the house?"

The children answered him: "O father dear!
God bless you, in captivity so long!
Your mother, whom we all love, is indoors.
But, father, tragedy had changed our lives –
Our mother dear, your wife, has passed away,
And yesterday we laid her in her grave."

They went into the house together then.
The mother of the Ban embraced her son:
"O Ban, my dearest son, light of my eyes –
My very eyes – I see the world through you!"

The Ban embraced his mother, then he said:
"My mother dear! Do not kiss only me –
But also kiss your daughter, my new bride!
This maiden freed me from my prison cell,
And she it was who brought me safely home."

THE BAN OF ZRIN

Praise be to God from whom all blessings flow!
There came to Zrin a letter from the Bey –
From Mustai-beg, the Bey of Novi town,
The letter was delivered to the Ban,
And this is what the writing in it said:
"My greetings to you, noble Ban of Zrin!
Return to me my horses, which you took!
Return to me my clothing, that you took!
Return my only sister, whom you took!
If you do not restore them all to me,
You shall receive a visit from me, Ban!"

The Ban did not obey: he took no heed.
But when the Holy Sabbath Day had dawned
The Ban led Begzada the maid to church,
And there she was baptized before the Cross.
Her name, from Begza, now to Katya changed,
The Ban then took her as his wedded wife.
Their union was blessed with progeny.
She bore to him three daughters and two sons.
And never did the Ban reproach his wife
That, as a maiden, she had been a Turk.

BALLADS OF
THE BORDER RAIDERS

26
Ivo Senkovich and the Aga of Ribnik

In Ribnik town the Turkish Aga sat.[1]
He wrote a letter to George Senkovich:[2]
"O mighty hero, O George Senkovich!
I have been told, and many men do say,
That as a warrior you have no peer –
But my companions say the same of me.
If it be true, George Senkovich, that you
Are doughty as a warrior, skilled at arms,
Then meet me on the field of honour here!
Fight me in single combat – prove your worth!
If you decline, then do a woman's work:
Knit me a woollen shirt and underclothes –
So shall I know that you submit to me!"

They brought the letter to George Senkovich.
He read it, and the tears flowed down his cheeks.
And Ivo Senkovich,[3] his son, cried out:
"My father dear, why do you shed these tears?
Before this day have many letters come
Into your hands, which you have read, and yet
Not one of them has caused your tears to flow."
George Senkovich, in sadness, answered him:
"O Ivo Senkovich, my dearest son!
'Tis true that many letters come to me
Which I have read, but this is not like them.
If such a one as this had come when I
Was in my youthful prime and full of strength,
I would have welcomed it and not shed tears.
From Ribnik's Aga has this letter come:
He calls on me to fight him to the death!
My son, you know that I am very old,
That I can barely sit my horse, still less

– 164 –

Could fight in single combat with the Turk.
And, as for knitting, I have never learned
To do it: I can't knit a shirt for him"

Then boldly Ivo Senkovich replied:
"George Senkovich, my father very dear!
I know full well that you are very old,
And could not fight a duel with the Turk.
But, when you prayed that you should have a son
God answered you: I am your gift from Him.
Now I shall go and meet this Turk, and fight
With him in single combat, in your stead."

George Senkovich most fondly answered him:
"O Ivo Senkovich, my dearest son!
Were you, my son, to go to fight with him
You would depart, but you would not return.
My son, you are still but an untried boy –
Not sixteen summers have you seen on Earth.
The Turk's a battle-hardened warrior
Whom none can match in all the Borderland.
And his appearance is most terrible –
He dresses all in lynx and sable fur,
His horse is covered in the hide of bears,
The skins of wolves enfold his battle-lance:
The sight of him will fill your heart with fear.
And when he shouts his battle-cry, and when
His battle-horse shrieks frienzedly, what then?
Your knees will turn to water, you will fall
In terror from your horse, and you'll be slain.
– What will then befall your grieving father?
Who will nourish, then, your aged parent?
Who, when he is dead, will see him buried?"

But Ivo Senkovich made straight reply:
"He will not scare me, father, by his dress.
A living wolf does not strike fear in me –

I am not frightened of a dead wolf's skin!
And if the fellow bellows like an ox –
I too can shout, as loud as any Turk.
Give me your leave and blessing, father dear,
To fight in single combat with this Turk.
I promise you, my father, whilst I live
You'll never have to knit a shirt for him"

 George Senkovich could not gainsay his son.
He saddled Doro, his bay battle-horse,
He saddled him, he kissed his mane, and said:
"O Doro mine, my very precious joy!
No more shall you and I go forth to war
To rescue captives from their Turkish bonds,
To strike off Turkish heads and bring them home.
For now, my Doro, I am growing old:
No longer can I wield a battle-lance.
I now entrust to you an innocent,
A beardless boy, Ivo, my only son.
O Doro, he is but a reckless lad –
Take care of him, and bring him safely back!"

 He then prepared his son most fittingly.
He dressed him in his own grand knightly garb,
He buckled his own sword on Ivo's belt
And then, in heartfelt tones, he blessed his son:
"O Ivo, Ivo, my own precious son!
Go now, and may good fortune go with you
Upon the road, and at your journey's end!
May God preserve you safe in life and limb,
May God protect you from your enemies,
From gaping wounds, and from the foeman's grasp.
Let your right hand and arm be firm and strong,
And let your sharpened sword strike hard and true!
Be sure you keep your eyes upon the Turk!
When you arrive at Ribnik, that fair town,

IVO SENKOVICH

Do not let fear assail your heart, my son!
But let your gaze be stern, your voice severe,
Your challenge to the Aga loud and clear!
And when you meet him on the battle-ground
Do not touch Doro with your goad or spur,
For I myself have trained him carefully:
He knows full well the skill and craft of war.
He will look after you and serve you well,
And he will save you from the Turk's sharp sword."

And Ivo, when he heard this blessing, knelt
And kissed his father on the hand and hem,
And kissed the ground on which his father stood.
He kissed his mother's hand and cried aloud:
"Dear parents, now forgive me, and farewell!"
Then Ivo mounted on his horse and as
He rode away he raised his voice in song:
His parents stayed. They watched him go, and wept.

When Ivo came to Ribnik there he saw,
Upon the plain, a fine pavilion.
Before it, battle-lances stood upright,
With mighty battle-horses hitched to them.
The Aga of Ribnik was sitting there
Beneath the tent, and drinking malmsey wine,
And sitting with him were two pasha's sons.
When Ivo's bay horse saw the other steeds
Its nostrils flared, it pawed the ground and neighed.

And seeing him, the pasha's sons cried out:
"My lord, Aga of Ribnik – see! Here comes
That ancient warrior George Senkovich.
O Aga, he will surely slay you now:
Today you will be parted from us all!"

But when the Aga looked at him who came,
And saw that it was Ivo Senkovich,
He said: "Dear brothers, do not be afraid!

That man who comes is not George Senkovich,
No – that is Ivo Senkovich, his son.
It was an evil choice his father made
To send his son to die a senseless death.
But, brothers, I've a mind to spare his life,
For he is nothing but a callow lad.
Instead, I'll capture him alive. They say
That George is very rich – he'll pay for him
A ransom of six wagon-loads of gold!"

   As thus the Aga spoke, Ivo approached
And, coming to the tent, addressed the Turks:
"O Turks of Ribnik, may God be with you!"
And, speaking civilly, the Turks replied:
"May God be with you, Ivo Senkovich!
You are most welcome, Ivo Senkovich!
What happy chance brings you before us now?"

   And Ivo Senkovich replied to them:
"Whoever is the Aga of Ribnik –
I challenge you in battle to the death!
Your letter to my father, calling him
To single combat, irritated me.
My father's very old, as you well know:
He is no longer fit to take the field,
But I am here to fight you in his stead."

   The Aga of Ribnik then softly said:
"Avoid the devil, and the battlefield,
Young Ivo! You have never seen a fight,
Still less have ever taken part in one.
But come, my friend, and drink good wine with us.
T'would be a shame to put an end to you
When you have spent so little time on Earth.
So, Ivo Senkovich, surrender now,
And let there be no death or bloody wounds!
And I do give my solemn word to you

That, in my hands, no harm shall come to you.
Besides, I know your father has great wealth,
He'll surely pay much gold to buy your life."

But Ivo Senkovich made straight reply:
"O Aga of Ribnik! I have not come
To put myself in thrall. No! – I have come
To measure strength and courage here with you,
O Turk, in single combat to the death!
Unless you are a woman, fight me now –
And do not waste more time in idle talk!"

The Aga hissed in rage, like any snake.
He leapt up to his feet and straightaway
He mounted on his great black battle-horse.
And then the Aga of Ribnik called out:
"Now, my fine hero, Ivo Senkovich!
Bestir your horse! You make the first attack!"

But Ivo Senkovich was wise. He said:
"Not so, O Turk, O Aga of Ribnik!
My horse is very weary: he and I
Have travelled far to come to you today.
I cannot make him charge: he has no strength.
But I will stand upon this very spot.
You stir your horse to frenzy – launch your charge!
I will not move from here, but will await
Your onslaught without flinching or retreat."

With this the Turk was very satisfied.
He made his horse to prance about the field;
He gripped his sharp and deadly battle-lance
And, like a mountain dragon, shouted out:
"Now have at you, O Ivo Senkovich!
Say not that there was any treachery!"

With that, the Aga charged across the field.
His battle-lance was aimed at Ivo's heart.
But Ivo's bay horse, Doro, dropped at once

SERBIAN EPIC BALLADS

Upon the grass – the lance flew overhead
And did not even brush Ivo's fur cap,
Still less did it do him an injury.
And Ivo Senkovich then swung his sword
And, with one blow, he smashed the Aga's lance.
At that the Aga saw that he was in
Great jeopardy, and that the fight was lost.
He turned his horse and fled away from him
And galloped like the wind towards Ribnik.
But Ivo spurred his horse and followed him.
The bay was not so tired, it seems! It soon
Drew level with the Aga's swift black horse –
Its head was by the Aga's horse's croup:
Its teeth were at the tassels on his belt.

The Aga, in his desperation, cried:
"God help me now: I am about to die!
Not killed in battle by a warrior
– Which would have been an honourable death –
But by that wondrous horse young Ivo rides!"

But Ivo was a young and foolish boy.
He should have killed the Aga with his sword;
He should have cut his head off, but instead
He tried to capture him alive. He thought
To take him to his father, as a prize.
The Turk recalled he had a hidden gun:
He drew it and, athwart his body, fired.
Thanks be to God! – the bullet missed Ivo,
But struck his horse between its jet-black eyes.
The horse, Doro, fell dead upon the grass,
But Ivo dropped upon his feet unharmed.

The Aga of Ribnik, when he saw this,
And saw that Ivo had no horse to ride,
Turned back and rode towards Ivo:
"What say you now, young Ivo Senkovich?

IVO SENKOVICH

What say you now? What hope is left for you,
Now I have parted you from your fine horse?
Surrender to me, Ivo Senkovich!
Captivity is better than the grave!"

But, like an angry serpent, Ivo hissed:
"O Aga of Ribnik! O mighty Turk!
I'll not surrender while I still have breath!
You may have parted me from my good horse:
You have not parted me from my good sword.
This is the very sword my father bore;
This sword has seen much battle and much war;
This sword has cut off many Turkish heads –
It will today, God willing, cut off yours!"

The Turk then, hissing like an angry snake,
Spurred on his horse and charged towards Ivo.
But Ivo showed he was a warrior bold.
He neither would avoid the Turk's attack,
Nor would he bend the knee to him,
But stood there, steadfast, as the Turk approached.
His sword flashed in his strong right hand,
He struck the Aga's horse – severed its head!
It fell and pinned the Aga to the ground.

And Ivo Senkovich then smiled at him:
"What say you now, O Aga of Ribnik?
What say you now? What hope is left for you?"

The Aga started to implore Ivo:
"In God's name, brother, Ivo Senkovich!
I beg of you to spare my life today.
I'll give you gold, as much as you desire!"

But sternly Ivo Senkovich replied:
"Your head is that which I desire the most –
Far more than all the riches of the Tsar."
He struck the Aga's head off with his sword
And put it in his horse's saddlebag.

In haste he stripped the Aga of his clothes –
He took them off and dressed himself in them.

  The two young pasha's sons had watched the fight
And saw the Aga of Ribnik was dead.
In bitterness and rage they shouted out:
"Our enemy must not remain alive:
Let us avenge our noble Aga's death!"
  They mounted battle-horses and set off
In hot pursuit of Ivo Senkovich.
And Ivo fled, like any hunted beast
Until, thank God, he reached the forest edge.
The Turks were foiled: the forest was too dense
For mounted men to follow one on foot.
So each dismounted from his battle-horse
And hitched it to a fir tree by its reins.
Together they pursued Ivo on foot.
But Ivo was no fool. He led the Turks
A merry dance, through bush and briar until,
While they still blundered after him, he came
To where the Turks had left their tethered steeds.
He loosed them, took their reins, and mounted one
The other one he led away, in tow,
And joyfully he shouted through the trees:
"My thanks to you, good Turks, for leaving me
These two fine battle-horses as a gift!"

  The two young pasha's sons heard this, and ran
To intercept Ivo upon the road.
They dared not leave the shelter of the woods
But, from the forest's edge, implored Ivo:
"In God's name, brother, Ivo Senkovich!
Those are two knightly horses. Bring them back –
Six hundred ducats will we pay for them!"
  But Ivo Senkovich called out to them:
"You speak in jest, you Turkish pasha's sons!

IVO SENKOVICH

I love these two fine battle-horses more
Than all the gold and treasure in Ribnik.
I cannot hunt you through these woods and so
You have no need of them! In any case,
I've left behind your Aga's horse and mine –
They were the best in all the Borderland!"

As Ivo homewards rode away, he sang.
The pasha's sons both watched him go, and wept.

When Ivo Senkovich drew near his home
His aged mother saw him, as he came.
She did not recognize her very son,
For he was wearing Turkish clothes and rode
A horse that she had never seen before.
She hissed in anguish, as a serpent does,
Her face went white: the tears flowed down her cheeks.
She ran inside her husband's noble hall:
"Oh, woe!" she cried, "O George, dear master, woe!
An evil thing it was to send your son
To fight in single combat in your stead.
Our Ivo's dead: he perished there! And now
The Aga of Ribnik himself has come
To burn and pillage and destroy our home,
And take away the two of us, dear George,
To serve the Turk as slaves in our old age!"

And when George Senkovich heard what she said
The tears flowed freely on his noble face.
But then he started up, and stood upright.
He buckled on his belt his shining sword.
He ran into the field where horses grazed
And seized an ancient mare. He had no time
To saddle her, or put a bridle on,
But, leaping up, he mounted her bare-backed
And flew across the plain towards Ivo.
He did not recognize his very son,

For he was wearing Turkish clothes, and rode
A horse that he had never seen before.

   George Senkovich in fury shouted out:
"Stop there, you coward, Aga of Ribnik!
It was an easy thing for you to kill
My son, a boy of less than sixteen years.
But now it is his father you must face!"
   But Ivo Senkovich cried eagerly:
"May God be with you, my dear father George!
I'm not the Aga of Ribnik: I am
Your own son, Ivo, O my father dear!"
   But, overwhelmed with grief and fury, George
Heard not a word of what Ivo had said.
He hurled himself upon his own dear son,
And made to cut his head off with his sword.
To what a dreadful pass has Ivo come!
He stands in mortal peril of his life,
About to perish at his father's hand!

   When Ivo saw that he would shortly die
He turned his back and made to flee away.
But George urged on his mare to follow him:
"Stop, Aga, stop!" he cried, "You'll not escape!"
   He rode so swiftly that he reached Ivo
And raised his sword to cut off Ivo's head.
When Ivo saw the peril he was in
He reached into his saddlebag in haste,
And seized the Aga's head. He pulled it out
And threw it down, right in his father's path:
"My father, for the love of God!" he cried,
"Behold! There's Ribnik's Aga! That's his head!"

   And when George recognized the Aga's face,
He pulled up sharp, and cast away his sword
Upon the grass. He leapt down from his mare
And went to Ivo's horse and halted it.

IVO SENKOVICH

He took the hand of Ivo, his own son,
He kissed him and embraced him tenderly:
"My dearest son, you have my deepest thanks
For doing that great deed instead of me,
Upholding so the honour of all men –
All people dwelling in the Borderland!
But why are you disguised in Turkish clothes?
You brought me to the verge of dreadful sin:
I came so close to killing you, my son!"

And Ivo Senkovich made this reply:
"George Senkovich, my father very dear!
How, otherwise, could I have proved that I
Had truly fought in single combat, when
I tell my tale to all the people here?
The gentlemen would not believe that I
Had fought and won in battle with the Turk,
Unless I had some souvenirs to show!"

27
Tadia Senyanin

It was the darkest hour before the dawn,
Before the Day-star yet had shown her face.
The gates of Sen[1] were opened and there passed
Through them a little band of warriors,
A company of four-and-thirty men.
Tadia Senyanin[2] was leading them;
The standard-bearer Komnen bore the flag.
They left the town and climbed up in the hills
And gathered near the place of Rufous Rocks.

   Tadia Senyanin then spoke to them:
"My brothers, friends, and good companions!
Is there no mother's son amongst you all
Who'll find a mountain shepherd in these hills
And get from him a ram of nine years old,
A good fat goat of seven years as well,
To make a supper for our company?"

   Now all the young men hung their heads in shame
And looked down at the dark earth fixedly.
But Yovan Kotarats did not look down.
He leapt up to his feet and went and found
A shepherd in the mountains with his flock.
From him he got a ram of nine years old,
A good fat goat of seven years as well,
And brought them back to where Tadia sat.
Then Tadia flayed both of them alive
And straightway drove them off, into the woods.
As brambles tore at them the goat screamed out:
The ram was silent, not a sound it made.

   Astonished, Yovan Kotarats cried out:
"O Tadia, our most respected chief!

Why flay those animals and let them go?"
Tadia Senyanin addressed them all:
"My friends and brothers, look at them! – mark well
The pain those animals are suffering.
But if the Turks should capture one of us
His pain will be more terrible by far!
My brothers dear, each one of you must learn
To suffer agony and make no sound,
Just like that wretched sheep before your eyes.
To anyone who cannot bear such pain
I say: 'Farewell! Let that man go with God;
He now must leave us and return to Sen.'"
So saying, Tadia leapt to his feet.
He seized his musket and, without delay,
Set off towards the place of Rufous Rocks.

Yovan Kotarats counted all the men,
But ten of them were missing; they had run
Away to Sen. Then Yovan said to him:
"O Tadia, why frighten everyone?
Ten men have left our band and fled away"
But Tadia Senyanin said to him:
"Dear brother Yovan, let the cowards go!
If they were such as trembled in great fear
To see the sight of one sheep flayed alive,
How would they stand tomorrow, at the sight
Of Hasan-aga Kuna, O my friend,
And of his thirty savage border-guards –
Each one of them aflame with lust to kill?"

But when they neared the place of Rufous Rocks
Yovan Kotarats counted heads once more –
And found that ten more men had fled away.
Once more Yovan Kotarats said to him:
"O Tadia, our most respected chief!
Why did you frighten all our thirty men? –

SERBIAN EPIC BALLADS

Ten more of them have left and fled away!"
But Tadia Senyanin said to him:
"My friend, Yovan Kotarats, let them go!
If they were such as trembled in great fear
To see the sight of one sheep flayed alive,
How would they stand tomorrow, at the sight
Of Hasan-aga Kuna, O my friend,
And of his thirty savage border-guards –
Each one of them aflame with lust to kill?"

But when they came at last to Rufous Rocks
Yovan Kotarats counted heads, and found
But one remained – Komnen who bore the flag.
Yovan Kotarats cried to Tadia:
"From thirty, only three of us are left!"
But Tadia Senyanin said to them:
"My good and faithful brothers, do not fear!
Provided that our hearts are strong and brave
There is no reason why the three of us
Can not fulfil the task of thirty men!"
The three then stopped and lay down for the night.

My friends, there was the sound and smell of fire
Deep in the woods, among the tall fir trees.
Tadia Senyanin said quietly:
"Amongst us is there not a mother's son
Who'll go and find out what men made that fire? –
They may be outlaws, or they may be Turks."

Komnen at once leapt up upon his feet
And took his musket firmly in his hand.
He edged his way between the forest trees
Until he came to where a camp fire burned
And through the trees he saw, around the fire,
A band of thirty Turks from Udbina,
With Hasan-aga Kuna in their midst:
And all were drinking wine and rakia.

When Hasan-aga Kuna took the cup
He raised it and he cried out to his men:
"Dearly beloved brethren, to your health!
Here's to you thirty men of Udbina!
And here's to Tadia Senyanin's head –
The heads of all his thirty bandits, too,
If God be willing! Let's all drink to that!"
Then, as they filled themselves with tawny wine,
They all got crazed with drink and fell about
Here, there, and everywhere, and went to sleep.
They left their muskets leaning on the trees.

Komnen the standard-bearer now crept forth.
He gathered all the Turks' slim muskets up
And went and hid them in the undergrowth.
He tried to take the Aga's sword, but it
Lay underneath his body as he slept.
So Komnen cut the Aga's belt, and then
He slipped the sword out from beneath the Turk,
And went back to Tadia Senyanin.

When he returned, Tadia questioned him:
"Well, Komnen, who is there? What did you see?
Who were they, gathered round the fire at night?"
Komnen the standard-bearer answered him:
"O Tadia, our much respected chief!
There's Hasan-aga Kuna by the fire,
And with him thirty men from Udbina.
They're all blind drunk and lying on the ground
Here, there, and everywhere, like logs, asleep.
I took their muskets, every one of them,
And hid them in the undergrowth nearby."

Tadia Senyanin believed him not
Until Komnen showed him the Aga's sword,
Which Tadia Senyanin recognised.
At once he led the others to the place

Where all the Turks lay round the fire asleep.
　Tadia laid the ambush on three sides:
On one side was Tadia Senyanin,
With standard-bearer Komnen opposite
And, on the third side, Yovan Kotarats.
And all of them had muskets primed and cocked.
　Then Tadia jumped up and ran across
To where the Aga lay in drunken sleep.
He kicked his arse and shouted in his ear:
"Get up, Hasan-aga Kuna, you swine!
Tadia Senyanin's come visiting,
With four and thirty of his friends beside,
To join you round your camp fire in the woods!"

　Kuna jumped up at once, aflame with rage,
And put his hand to draw his shining sword.
But when he saw it was no longer there
He looked to get assistance from his men.
They ran to get their muskets – all in vain;
Their fine slim muskets were no longer there.
　Then Tadia Senyanin shouted out:
"Stand still, Hasan-aga Kuna, you swine!
We have your weapons, every one of them.
Now go! Tie up your thirty border-guards,
Or otherwise, I promise faithfully,
Our thirty muskets all will fire at once,
And then I'll tie their bodies up myself."

　When Kuna saw there was no hope for him
He slowly went, reluctantly, and bound
The hands of all his thirty border-guards:
He tied the bonds and Komnen tightened them.
The Aga bound the thirty border-guards,
And Komnen bound the Aga's hands himself.
And then they went into the undergrowth
And brought out all the muskets of the Turks.

TADIA SENYANIN

They slung the Turkish muskets on their backs,
And then they drove the Turks, the three of them,
They drove the thirty Turkish border-guards,
They drove them down to Sen in Krayina,

   And when they came before the gates of Sen
The people, great and small, in wonder stared.
The girls and maidens sang aloud in glee:
"Dear God be praised: a wondrous miracle!
That three good men of Sen could, all alone,
Defeat and capture thirty cruel Turks,
And suffer neither death nor wounds themselves!"
Tadia Senyanin called back to them:
"It was no miracle, you pretty girls!
Good fortune and misfortune met by chance:
The luck was on my side but not on theirs,
Good luck and bad are ever intertwined."

   And after that they threw the thirty Turks
Into the dungeons underneath the keep.
They held the Turks and ransomed them for gold:
And three and thirty bags of gold they fetched.
To Tadia Senyanin came the gold.
But then the mother of Tadia came
And spoke these words to Tadia, her son:
"O Tadia, my son, dost thou not know –
It was at Kuna's hands thy father died?"

   And when Tadia Senyanin heard this,
He kept three bags of gold, the rest returned.
He then released the thirty captive Turks,
Holding his sword aloft as each passed by.
   But when bold Hasan-aga Kuna passed
The sword descended: he struck off his head.

BALLADS OF
THE MONTENEGRINS

28
The Three Prisoners

Imprisoned by the Pasha of Skadar,[1]
Three Montenegrin chieftains cursed their fate.
The Pasha held them all as hostages
Against the tax upon the mountain folk.
The highlanders were proud, and stiff of neck:
They would not pay the poll tax on the clans.

   The Pasha had deceived these noblemen;
He lured them to his fort with honeyed words,
But when they came he flung them into gaol.

   The first was Vuksan of the Rovchani,[2]
The second Liyesh of the Piperi,
The third of them Selak Vasoyevich.
Most bitterly they cursed: captivity
Was hardly to be borne by mountain-men.

   Now Vuksan spoke. He asked the other two:
"My brothers dear, and good companions,
We know full well that we are here to die.
Well, so be it! What causes you most grief?"

   And Liyesh of the Piperi replied:
"My greatest grief, my brothers, lies in this –
I am a young man, and but briefly wed.
I leave behind a wife in my fair hall
Whom I have barely known, caressed, or loved,
Or chided, even, or have made my own.
That is the cause of greatest grief to me."

   Selak Vasoyevich was next to speak:
"My greatest grief, my brothers, lies in this –
I have at home much land and property,
I have, as well, uncounted stores of gold,
And in the hills I have a thousand sheep.

My mother will be left without a son;
My sister left without a brother's care.
And they will wail and weep in misery,
Within my fine and noble palace walls."

But then spoke Vuksan of the Rovchani:
"My brothers, no true hero grieves for such!
I, too, have lands and property at home.
My mother, too, will lose her only son.
I, too, have scarcely come to know my wife.
My dearest sister, too, is still unwed.
I do not grieve for any of those things.
What grieves me most – it rends my heart – is that
I die without the chance to wreak revenge!"

And after them, another voice was heard:
It was the Pasha's executioner,
Who stood outside that loathsome prison's door.
He called Liyesh the Voivoda by name:
"Voivoda Liyesh of the Piperi!
Come out of that dark cell: you shall go free!
The Piperi have paid your ransom price.
They've handed over all their flocks of sheep,
And brought uncounted stores of treasure, too,
And also one fair maiden, as a slave."

And so was Voivoda Liyesh deceived.
He left the prison cell, and came outside.
The executioner drew out his sword.
He cut Liyesh's head off with one blow
And threw his corpse behind the prison wall.

And after that the executioner
Returned, and stood outside the prison door.
He called Selak Vasoyevich by name:
"O Voivoda Selak Vasoyevich!
Come out of that dark cell: you shall go free!
Your aged mother's here, and she has come

To pay the ransom and redeem her son.
She's handed over many cows and bulls,
And fat white sheep and little lambs beside
And, more than that, uncounted stores of gold."

And so was Voivoda Selak deceived.
He left the prison cell and came outside.
The executioner drew out his sword.
And with one blow he cut off Selak's head
And threw his corpse behind the prison wall.

The executioner returned again
And stood outside the prison door and called.
He called the name of Voivoda Vuksan:
"O Vuksan of the Rovchani, come out!
Your clan has paid your ransom: you are free!
They've paid for you in treasure, two great chests,
And both are full of gold Venetian coins.
And also many sheep and lambs they've brought;
An unwed maiden as a slave, besides."

But Vuksan, like a cunning deadly snake,
Was not deceived by what the Turk had said.
He left the prison cell and came outside,
And spoke to him in even tones. He said:
"Sir Executioner, a moment, pray!
Untie my hands, and let me first take off
This grand and costly clothing that I wear.
This fine green dolman must come off my back,
For under it are gold medallions.
Three pounds each weighs, in Venice all were struck,
Five hundred ducats is the worth of them.
And under them I have a shirt of gold.
It was not made of ordinary cloth,
Or woven on an ordinary loom –
A mountain spirit gave this shirt to me:
To ruin it with blood would be a shame!"

THE THREE PRISONERS

   The Turk was gullible: he coveted
The shirt of gold. He untied Vuksan's hands.
But Vuksan did not take his dolman off –
He grabbed the executioner's own sword
And hacked the fellow's head off with one blow!
And then he fled away through Skadar town.

   There thirty men-at-arms were on alert,
Determined quickly to recapture him.
But Vuksan was not willing to be caught.
He swung the sword, and slashed to left and right,
And cut the heads off all the thirty Turks –
Then onward rushed in frantic headlong flight.

   He reached the bridge across the Boyana.
A kadi[3] and a hodja[4] waited there.
They stood upon the bridge and sternly said:
"No further forward, Voivoda Vuksan!
No further forward, or you lose your head!"
   But Voivoda Vuksan replied to them:
"Kadi and hodja, hear me, both of you!
If I can not go forward on my way,
I neither can go back the way I came!"
   His sharp sword flashed: he cut off both their heads,
And threw the corpses in Boyana's stream,
And rushed on, ever forward, in his flight.

   They hunted him with soldiers, horse and foot.
The horsemen barely caught a glimpse of him:
The men on foot had neither sight nor sound.
At last he came alive to his own hills.

   So he escaped, and gave his mother joy.
Her joy's in him: my joy's in you, my friends.

29

How they took Beg Lyubovich's Sheep

There came a small patrol of fighting men.[1]
As was their wont, they formed a company
From Kichevo,[2] among the border hills.
Two captains were the leaders of that band:
The first of them was Rade Baletich,
The second was Niko Tomanovich.
To Hercegovina they marched until
They reached Nevesinye[3] and there they found
A bounteous prize: Beg Lyubovich's sheep.
They rounded up his flocks, left none behind,
And drove them out of Hercegovina.

But when they reached the plain of Rudiné,[4]
Another company of men appeared,
A company from Nikshich, that fair town.[5]
Two Turkish captains[6] led that company,
And Sever Piper was the name of one,
Muyo Arivovich the other's name.
They also came to Rudine, and saw
The company of men from Kichevo –
The company of Rade Baletich,
With all the sheep that they were driving off.

The Turkish leader cried out to his men:
"My Turkish brethren, in the name of God!
Let no man fire upon that murderer
Niko Tomanovich, the very man
Who killed my brother born – leave him to me!"
The company obeyed their leader's words:
They lay in ambush by the grassy track.

They waited till Niko approached, and then
Their leader raised his musket, and he fired.

The bullet was well aimed: it struck Niko,
But hit the metal buttons on his coat,
And did not penetrate to pierce his skin!
   Niko at once fired back: his luck was in!
His shot was truly aimed: it found its mark –
His bullet struck the Turk between the eyes!
When Rade Baletich saw what was done
He shouted to the young man by his side:
"Now run, my nephew Zhivko, and make haste –
Bring back that Turk's fine musket, and his head!"

   Zhivko at once ran over to the Turk
To get his weapon and cut off his head.
But close to him there was another Turk,
Who raised his musket, aimed, and fired at him.
His aim was true: the bullet hit him square.
It blew away his heart and Zhivko fell,
But, as he died, through gritted teeth he cried:
"Make haste, my uncle, Rade Baletich!
Come! Take my musket – take my head as well,
So that the Turks may not get hold of them!"

   And now the Turk who'd shot Zhivko leapt out
And rushed towards him, fast as he could run,
To seize his musket, and cut off his head.
But Rade Baletich had seen him come:
He aimed and fired his fine Italian gun.
His aim was true: his bullet hit the Turk
Full in the chest and tore his heart away.
The Turk fell dead on Zhivko's lifeless corpse.
Then Rade Baletich ran up to them
And took away their heads and muskets, both.

   At that the other Turks all turned their backs
And fled away across Rudine's plain.
The Montenegrin lads ran after them:
They caught them, and they cut off all their heads,

And seized the weapons they were carrying.
So all of them took trophies: each one had
A Turk's head, and a Turkish musket too.

And then they went upon their homeward path,
Still driving all the sheep that they had seized.
And when at last they came to Kichevo,
They shared the booty out in amity,
And each of them went safely to his home.

May God preserve us all for evermore!

BALLADS OF THE
NINETEENTH-CENTURY
UPRISINGS

30

The Start of the Revolt against the Dahiyas

Dear God, what great and wondrous happenings!
When in the Serbian lands there first swelled up
The tide of change that swept away the Turks,
And saw the realm of Serbia restored.
It was not done by princes waging war,
Nor did the Turkish gluttons wish for it.
The hungry common people[1] of the land
Arose – they could no longer pay the tax,
Nor bear the threefold burden of the Turks.
For all those who were blessed by God were roused –
The blood began to boil up through the earth.
They knew the time had come for waging war,
The time to shed their blood for Christianity,
And to avenge their ancestors at last.

In heaven the very Saints were battling,
And sending signs and portents in the bright
And cloudless sky that arches over Serbia.
And of these wondrous signs this was the first:
From Tripun's Day to that of Holy George
Each night the moon was darkened by eclipse,
To tell the Serbs to rise up under arms –
But they were sore afraid, and did not rise.

The Saints in heaven sent a second sign:
From George's Day to Saint Dimitri's Day
Came comets, bloody banners in the bright
And cloudless sky that arches over Serbia,
To tell the Serbs to rise up under arms –
But they were sore afraid, and did not rise.

A third portent the Saints in heaven sent:
The thunder rumbled on Saint Sava's Day,
In deepest winter, when it thunders not.

SERBIAN EPIC BALLADS

Upon the Day of Peter's Chains the lightning flashed,
And earthquakes shook the land from west to east,
To tell the Serbs to rise up under arms –
But they were sore afraid, and did not rise.

A fourth portent the Saints in heaven sent:
For in the clear and cloudless sky the sun
Itself, that Spring, was hesitant to rise.
In Spring, upon Saint Tripun's Day,
There were three dawnings at the break of day;
That day the sun rose three times in the east!

The Turks in Belgrade City saw these signs.
All seven of the Dahiyas were there:[2]
Aganliya and Kuchuk Aliya,
Beside them there were Focho's two young sons,
Memed-aga and Mus-aga by name,
And Mula Yusuf, mighty Dahiya,
And Dervish-aga, Town Provisioner,
And old Focho, the centenarian.

They met together, seven Dahiyas,
Beside the Stambol Gate of old Belgrade,
And all were dressed in fur-tipped scarlet cloaks.
They saw the wondrous portents, and they cried:
"Alas, my brothers, these are troubled times:
These things, my comrades, bode not well for us!"

And then, in fear, the seven Dahiyas
Took up a bowl of crystal glass and went
To fill it from the Danube's flowing stream.
They took the water to Neboysha's Tower,
Climbed to the top, and there set down the bowl.
They gazed down at the image of the stars
Upon the water's surface. There they sought
For mystic signs, their future to foretell.
And as the Dahiyas stood round the bowl
They all leaned over it. They thought to see

Their own reflections on the water's face.
They looked on it, but nothing did they see –
Nor head, nor face, of any one of them!

    They took an axe of steel and with it smashed
The bowl of crystal glass, and then they threw
The broken fragments from the tower's height
Into the Danube River, where they sank,
So that the bowl might nevermore be used.

    And after that the seven Dahiyas,
Now driven by anxiety and fear,
Descended from Neboysha's Tower in haste
And made their way, together, to an inn.
And there, within a meeting-room, they sat
In order of their seniority –
The venerable Focho at their head,
His long white beard falling to his waist.
The seven Dahiyas then shouted out:

    "Attend upon us, all you priests and seers!
Make haste! And bring with you the holy books.
And read those books, and tell us what they say
Shall be our future and our destiny!"

    The priests and seers gathered in the hall;
They brought with them the sacred holy books.
And when they read the books, they wept great tears,
And thus, in grief, addressed the Dahiyas:

    "O brother Turks, O seven Dahiyas!
These are the sayings of the holy books:
When last such signs and portents did appear
Within the clear skies over Serbia
– Five hundred years have passed away since then –
They marked the time the Serbian realm was lost,
And we assumed the power and government.
The Tsars who ruled the infidels we slew:
Tsar Constantine was slain in Tsarigrad[3]

REVOLT AGAINST THE DAHIYAS

Beside the icy waters of Sharats,
And Tsar Lazar was slain at Kosovo,
Where Milosh[4] struck Murat a mortal blow.
But Milosh did not kill him with that stroke,
For Murat lived until the day was won
– The day on which we took the Serbian realm –
And with his dying breath, he spoke these words:
   'O brother Turks! Vezirs and Generals!
Now I must die; the empire falls to you.
Hear what I say; you must obey my words,
So that your rule may last a thousand years.
Do not be cruel to the Serbian folk;
Do right to them, and be considerate.
If fifteen dinars be the hearth-tax rate,
Or even thirty dinars, so be it.
Do not then levy fines and penalties
As well: do not bleed white the common folk.
Do not despoil their churches, disrespect
Their Faith, or trample on their dignity.
Inflict no vengeance on the Serbian folk.
As for this wound that Milosh dealt to me –
Such is the fortune of the warrior's trade.
You cannot take an empire at your ease,
Or lying on a sofa, dreaming dreams.
You must not persecute the common folk,
And drive them to take refuge in the hills;
Look after them as though they were your sons.
So shall your empire last a thousand years.
But if you do not hearken to my words,
And if you drive the people to revolt,
Then you will lose the empire we have won.'
   So Murat died, and we remained to rule.
But we did not obey his dying words.
We laid upon the folk a crushing tax,
We rode rough-shod upon their dignity,

We drove them into penury most dire,
We pressed upon them fines and penalties,
Despoiled their churches, trampled on their pride.
   Now, once again, the portents have appeared:
Those signs that tell an empire is to end.
It is not any king that you need fear.
Against an emperor no king prevails –
No kingdom can an empire overthrow,
For God has made the world in such a way.
But now beware the starving Serbian folk!
For when the hoes and mattocks rise and fall,
Then Turks as far as Medina shall quake,
And Turkish women weep in Syria –
The common folk shall bring them great distress.
   O Turks! O brothers! Seven Dahiyas!
This is what the holy books have told us:
All our houses shall be burnt by fire.
You, the Dahiyas, shall all be slaughtered.
Grass shall grow up through our ruined hearth-stones.
All our empty mosques shall harbour cobwebs.
No more shall be heard the call to prayer.
Everywhere, upon our roads and highways
– Thronged with Turkish travellers and ringing
With the clattering hooves of many horses –
Weeds and grass shall sprout between the cobbles.
Vainly shall the roads await our passing:
Turks shall not be found within this country.
   These are the sayings of the holy books."

   And when the seven Dahiyas heard that,
All seven sat in silence, eyes downcast.
They gazed upon the ground in front of them;
Not one of them could find a fitting word
To contradict the sayings of the books.
The venerable Focho stroked his beard
And ground his teeth together silently.

REVOLT AGAINST THE DAHIYAS

He could not contradict the holy books,
But sat in silence, and in wonderment.

But Memed-aga would not hold his peace.
He broke the silence – stridently he cried:
"Begone! Depart, you priests and seers all!
Go and say your prayers, and call the Faithful
Five times every day to say their prayers!
Do not concern yourselves with us, the Dahiyas,
So long as all of us are wise and strong,
And whilst we hold the City of Belgrade –
And we are capable of holding it
Against the common people all around,
For if they have no chiefs to challenge us
How shall this rabble do us any harm?
Lo! There are seven of us Dahiyas;
Each one of us possesses treasure-stores.
What kind of treasure? – golden ducats all!
And all that treasure's lying idle there.

My brothers! Just between the four of us –
Aganliya and Kuchuk Aliya,
And I, and Mula Yusuf, just ourselves,
Have massive, overflowing stores of gold
Uncountable, in two great treasuries.
And if the four of us combine at once,
And all of us stand firm, courageously,
We can, by opening our treasure-stores
And scattering Venetian ducats everywhere,
Recruit as many soldiers as we want.
Then can we four, we mighty Dahiyas,
Divide our army into four brigades
Of equal size, as brothers share alike.
Then shall we leave the city in great force,
And purge the districts round, all seventeen.
We shall kill their princes and their chieftains:
All the Serbian leaders we shall slaughter –

Headmen too, as many as is needful –
Priests, who teach the Serbs defiance, also.
Nothing shall we leave alive but children –
Silly children, infants under seven.
That will fill the common folk with terror –
After that they'll serve us Turks most humbly.

Until I kill the knez[5] Palaliya
From Begalyitsa, that small, pretty town -
He is a pasha, I'm an underling.

Until I also kill Yovan the knez
Of Landov village – pretty place it is –
He is a pasha, I'm an underling.
And Stanoye, of Zeok town the knez,
He is a pasha, I'm an underling.

Until I kill knez Stevo Yakovlyev
Of Liyevach, that outlaws' rookery,
He is a pasha, I'm an underling.
And also Yovan, knez of Kersnitsa.

Until I kill the Charapichi, both,
Beside the stream that flows from Avala,
– For both of them could come upon Vrachar
And block our Turkish force inside Belgrade –
They are the pashas, I'm an underling.

Until I kill that bandit Karageorge[6]
Of Topola,[7] that nest of renegades,
– Who's trading with the Austrian Emperor,
Who's buying arms and ammunition in
The town of Varadin, and storing them,
With many other weapons; who alone
Is capable of waging war on us –
He rules as king, and I'm an underling.

Until I also kill the high priest Nikola
From Ritopek, another pretty town,
He is a pasha, I'm an underling.

Until I kill the hero Djordjiye,

And Arseniya, his own brother born,
From Zhelyeznik, that village fair and fine;
He could deny the route to Topchider.

Until I kill that Marko, the high priest
Of Ostruzhnitsa village where he lives,
He is a pasha, I'm an underling.

Until I kill those Archimandrites two –
Adji-Djera, and Adji-Ruvim, both,
Who know well how to melt down gold,
And how to write deceiving missives to
The Sultan, slandering us, the Dahiyas,
And get the common folk to worship them –
They are the pashas, we are underlings.

Until I kill Iliya Birchanin
The obor-knez[8] from under Medjenik:
– Who, without cease, throughout the last three years
Has steadily increased his strength and power,
And who now rides a fine great dappled horse,
And takes a second one where'er he goes,
And hangs a bludgeon from his saddle-bow;
Has black moustaches and a great black hat,
And who forbids his district to the Turks.
If one should stray within his boundaries
He hits him with his bludgeon – breaks his ribs;
And if a Turk within his district dies,
He calls upon his bandit followers:
'My servants, throw this carrion to the dogs,
Where ravens will not find his bones to pick!'
And when he brings the tax-money to me
He comes into my presence under arms.
He holds his sabre's hilt in his right hand,
And gives me the tax-money with his left.
'Memed-aga,' he says, 'Here are your dues!
The starving folk present their compliments,
But nothing further can you squeeze from them.'

And when I start to count the pile of coins
His glaring eyes are like two daggers drawn.
'Memed-aga,' he says, 'No need for that!
I have, myself, already counted them.'
And then I can no longer count the cash,
But have to throw the money to one side.
I cannot wait to see the end of him
Because I cannot look him in the face –
He is a pasha, I'm an underling.

    Until I execute knez Gerbovich
Of Mratishich, that village fine and fair,
He is a pasha, I'm an underling.

    Until I execute knez Aleksa
Who comes from that fair town, Brankovina,
Along with him his brother Yakov, too
– For when the Sultan fought the Emperor
Of Austria they served the Emperor,
And finished, both, with helmets full of gold,
By plundering the Turkish provinces.
They pillaged all of them, and burnt the towns.
But when the Sultan and the Emperor
Made peace, those turncoats both changed sides, and then
Became officials in the Sultan's pay,
And many Turkish citizens betrayed.
They slandered seven pashas with their false
Reports, and executed all of them –
Still they are pashas, we are underlings.

    Until I kill the Tavna district chief,
The obor-knez Stanko from Lyutitsa;
And until I kill the knez of Machva,
Lazar Martinovich from Bogatich,
They are the pashas, I'm an underling.

    And also, till I kill the knez of Potseryé,
Mihailo Ruzhichich from Metkovich,
He is a pasha, I'm an underling.

REVOLT AGAINST THE DAHIYAS

Until I burn Racha, on Drina's bank,
And kill therein Adji-Melentiye
– Who travelled far across the azure sea,
And visited the shrine of infidels,
Who went to see the Sultan in Stambol[9]
And by deception wheedled out of him
A warrant for a hundred ducats for
The building of a church for infidels.
Construction was to last for seven years:
Twelve months were all he took to finish it.
And for the last six years, all round the church,
He has been building military walls,
And in the walls embrasures he has made,
And secretly has mounted guns in them.
You see, my comrades, what he hopes to do!

Through every district, therefore, I shall go,
And kill the Serbian headmen, every one.
That done, how can the rabble injure us?"

The Dahiyas all leapt up to their feet,
Applauding Memed-aga in these words:
"Our thanks to you, Fochich-Memed-aga!
For you have shown more sense than all of us.
Our leader you shall be: we all agree
To follow you – you have but to command!"

But then the venerable Focho spoke:
"Behold a young man, with a young man's head!
How will he hold the kingdom by such means?
My dear son, Fochich-Memed-aga, think!
What happens if you take a bunch of straw,
And start to beat a burning fire with it –
What will you do? Will you put out the fire?
Or will you cause the flames to burn more bright?
You have the power, which God has given you,
To buy as many soldiers as you want,

And ravage all the districts – that you can.
A single headman you may well seduce,
And bring him to his doom by wily words,
But then your credibility is gone.
You can kill one, but two will then arise;
You kill those two, and four will then spring up,
And they will burn your houses to the ground,
And slaughter all of you, the Dahiyas.
But this is not the way that you should go.

Hear what I say: I am your senior!
I, too, have listened to the sacred texts;
Our downfall need not follow from their words.
They tell of change, of change of governance.
My son, you must relieve the common folk,
You must take off the burden from their backs:
Reduce the tax to that which Murat set.
Abolish all the fines and penalties.
Befriend each Serbian headman, and each knez.
Give him a gift – an Arab stallion,
And to his deputy a working-horse;
Be friendly to their priests and ministers.
So may we live in peace with all of them!
For otherwise our reign will soon be done,
And then what profit lies in your great wealth?
If it were grain, you could not eat it all."

But Fochich-Memed-aga shouted out:
"My father, you are old: I hear you not!"

And with these words he leapt up to his feet,
And with him all the other Dahiyas.
They set up cannon on the city walls;
Recruited soldiers, paying them in gold.
All this was done by four great Dahiyas:[10]
Mula Yusuf, Fochich-Memed-aga,
Aganliya, and Kuchuk Aliya.
The army they divided in four corps

Of equal size, as brothers share alike.
Then, opening the gates, they all marched out
To scour the countryside and there inflict
Harsh punishment upon the Serbian folk.

   The first whom they encountered was the knez
Palaliya: to him they spoke fair words,
And then, at Grotska, executed him.
And Stanoye, the knez of Zeok town
They first deceived, and then put him to death
Within the very walls of his own house.

   They spoke fine words to Marko Charapich;
Soft words they spoke, and then they murdered him.
Commander Yanko Gagich was the next
To die, within the village of Bolech.

   They killed knez Teofan of Orashye
In Smederevo district, and they killed
There also knez Petar of Resava.

   Commander Mata, chief at Lipovats
Near Kraguyevats – him they first seduced
With lying words, then executed him.

   The church at Moravitse they attacked,
And there they took and killed Adji-Djera.
Adji-Ruvim they captured, and took him
To Belgrade City, where they murdered him.[11]

   Then Memed-aga went to Valyevo
For Gerbovich, but he had been forewarned,
And Gerbovich had safely fled away.
But obor-knez Aleksa came to him;
There also came Iliya Birchanin,
And Memed-aga seized the pair of them.
He bound their noble hands, and led them both
Upon the Kolubara river bridge.

   And when the Obor-knez Aleksa saw
That now the Turks were going to kill them both,
He spoke to Memed-aga in these words:

"My lord, Fochich-Memed-aga! Grant me
The gift of single combat for my life.
See! I will pay you sixty bags of gold!"

But Memed-aga said to Aleksa:
"Your life I will not grant you, Aleksa,
Nor would I for a hundred bags of gold."

Then Iliya Birchanin said to him:
"My gracious lord, Fochich-Memed-aga!
See! I will pay a hundred bags of gold:
Grant me the gift of combat for my life!"

But Fochich-Memed-aga said to him:
"What foolishness, Iliya Birchanin!
No one would free a ravening mountain-wolf!"

Then Memed called the executioner.
The executioner drew forth his sword
And with one blow struck off Iliya's head.

Then Aleksa sat down upon the bridge
And started loudly to declaim these words:
"May God forbid that any Christian man
Should ever place his trust in any Turk!
My brother Yakov! O, my brother born!
Beware the Turks! Beware their blandishments!
Where'er you find them, strike them to the ground ..."

But Aleksa could speak no further words:
The executioner would hear no more –
The sword-blade flashed as he struck off his head.

And in the hour that those two princes died
Upon the Kolubara river bridge
– Knez Aleksa and Iliya Birchanin –
So also, in that hour, Adji-Ruvim
Was murdered in Belgrade. And in that hour
The shining sun was darkened in the sky.
And Memed-aga scurried to his home
Instead of looking for more Serbs to kill,
Or choosing someone else to execute.

REVOLT AGAINST THE DAHIYAS

But when the Serbs received this dreadful news
They fled away from towns and villages
And hid; none came to Memed-aga more.
And when Fochich-Memed-aga saw this
He knew at once that worse was bound to come,
And bitterly repented of his acts,
But also knew repentance came too late.

    He called together twelve young bodyguards,
His adjutant Uzun also, and said:
"Now listen to me well, my brave young hawks!
Make haste! Now saddle up and mount your steeds,
And ride at once to Topola, and there
Find Karageorge, and make an end of him.
And if you let Black George escape, then know
That you yourselves shall pay a heavy price!"

    And when the twelve young guardsmen heard these words,
They saddled up their battle-horses, and
With adjutant Uzun in charge, and leading them,
They rode away and went to Topola.
'Twas Saturday, upon the Sabbath's eve.

On Sunday morning, in the silent hours
Before the dawn, before bright day had come,
They came to Karageorge's house, and they
Surrounded it and aimed their guns at it
From two directions, then they shouted out:
"George Petrovich, awake! Come out of there!"

But who shall take a serpent unaware,
Or who shall catch it sleeping in its lair?
For Karageorge was shrewd; his habit was
To be awake before the day had dawned,
To wash himself, and say his morning prayers,
And drink a little glass of rakia.
So, he had risen early on this day,
And gone out to the sheds below the house.

He saw the Turks surround his house, and he
Did not reveal himself to them, but watched.
And then his wife came out and spoke to them:
"May God be with you, Turks, it still is night!
What are you doing at this early hour?
My husband George was here, before the house –
I saw him there – but he has gone away,
And I know not at all where he has gone."
All this was seen and heard by Karageorge.

When Karageorge had counted up the Turks,
He drank a dram, and then prepared his gun.
He took a stock of powder and of ball,
And to his stockyard went, in secrecy,
To speak to his twelve herdsmen sleeping there.
As soon as he arrived he wakened them,
And calling them around him, spoke to them:
"My brothers all, you twelve good men and true!
Get up at once! Open the stockyard gates,
Rouse out the pigs, and drive them out of there –
Just let them go and forage where they will.
But you, my brothers, follow and obey
My orders. Load your muskets – prime them well!
If God allows, and should He bless the work
That we shall undertake this very day,
Much honour shall each one of you receive.
Much gold and silver shall be your reward,
And you shall dress in silk and velvet clothes!"

The herdsmen all were eager to obey.
They roused the pigs, and drove them from the yard.
Their guns they loaded, and they primed them well,
And then fell in, to follow Karageorge.

They all went straight to Karageorge's house,
And when they saw the Turks surrounding it
George gave his orders – this is what he said:

"Now listen to me, my twelve herdsmen true!
Let all of you take aim at one Turk each,
But hold your fire, and do not shoot your man
Until you see and hear me fire my gun.
I shall take aim at adjutant Uzun,
And we shall see what luck I have with him!"

And when George Petrovich had spoken thus,
He lay down on the ground and took good aim.
He fired his gun; the others held their fire.
Where George had aimed his shot went, straight and true,
And Uzun fell dead from his dappled horse.
Then, when the herdsmen saw what George had done,
They opened fire at once, all twelve of them.
Six of the Turks fell dead upon the ground,
The other six, still mounted, fled away.

Then George at once went all round Topola
Collecting other men to join his band,
And all the company pursued the Turks
Into Sibnitsa village, where they fled.
And there the Turks sought refuge in an inn,
As if to shelter in their mothers' laps!
But George and all his men surrounded it,
And then he called the men of Sibnitsa.
They came at once, and joined his company –
By now there were a hundred men with him.
When they arrived they set fire to the inn,
And of the Turks, three burnt to death inside.
The other three escaped the flames and ran;
The Serbs pursued and killed them, every one.

And now did Karageorge send messages
To all the district chiefs in Serbia,
And all the village headmen in the land:
"Kill all the Turkish deputies, spare none!
The women and the children, hide away!"

And when the Serbian chieftains heard this call
They all did that which Karageorge had said.
They all arose, they leapt up to their feet;
They buckled on their weapons, and they hid
The women and the children in the woods,
And then they killed the Turkish deputies.

When Karageorge had roused all Serbia,
And started the revolt against the Turks,
Through all the districts, then, he went about.
He burned the Turkish watchtowers to the ground;
He smashed the fair pavilions of the Turks,
And devastated all their settlements.
He burnt the Turkish villages entire:
The men and women put he to the sword.
The Serbs would show no mercy to the Turks.

   The Turks thought lightly of the common folk,
But now the folk were masters of the land.
They grew up from the earth as grows the grass,
And spread like grass, invading all the towns.

Now Karageorge went forth to every town
Which housed a Turkish garrison, and called:
"Now hear me well, you citizens within!
Do not delay: open your city gates.
Send out the Turkish tyrants from the town!
Obey me if you wish to live in peace,
And if you do not wish to be destroyed!
For if you do not send them out at once –
Those Turks who wield the power in the town –
Remember who it was that built your towns!
The common folk took nine years building them:
The common folk can smash them in a day,
And stand their ground in battle with the Turks.
For we are all prepared and fit for war.
And if the seven kings all rise at once

REVOLT AGAINST THE DAHIYAS

To pacify us, they will find no peace,
For we shall fight and die till none are left!"

At this the citizens wept bitter tears,
And in these words they answered Karageorge:
"Prince Karageorge, Master of Serbia!
We'll give to you whate'er your people want.
We beg of you, do not destroy our towns!
We beg you, do not visit war on us!
We'll send the Turkish tyrants out to you!"

And in each town the citizens rose up
And opened wide the city gates to him.
They seized the Turkish lords and sent them out
– Those grasping, gluttonous, and greedy Turks –
Surrendered all of them to Serbian hands.

To God and to His Mother thanks and praise!
For when the Serbian people seized those Turks,
And had the greedy tyrants in their hands,
They drove them forth, upon the open fields,
Without their clothing and their silken shirts,
Without their fur-lined hats and overcoats,
Without their turbans wound around their heads,
Without their kerchiefs, and without their shoes.
They beat them, naked, barefoot, and they cried:
"How now, fine Sirs! What price our taxes now!"

Then Karageorge went forth with naked sword
And cut the head off every one of them.

But though George cut the heads off many Turks,
It was the Turkish tyrants that he culled.
For after that he went into the towns,
And in those towns, as many Turks there were,
So many Turks for harvesting, he took;
As many were for saving, those he saved;
As many sought baptism, were baptised.

When Karageorge had taken Serbia,
And once again restored the Christian Faith,
And brought the people all beneath his wing –
Serbian folk, from Vidin to the Drina,[12]
And all from Kosovo to fair Belgrade –
He gazed upon the Drina, and he said:
"O River Drina, noble boundary
Dividing Bosnia from Serbia!
The time will come, and it will not be long,
Before I pass across your flowing stream
And step on honourable Bosnia's soil!"

APPENDIX

Notes on the Ballads

General: Brief descriptions of most of the bards named in the Notes, and of Vuk Karadžić and his work, appear in the Introduction, section two.

1
Tsar Dushan's Wedding (*Ženidba Dušanova*)

This version of a famous ballad was dictated to Vuk Karadžić by the bard whom he considered to be the finest of his age, Tešan Podrugović. As with many 'wedding' ballads, this one is used not only as a description of pageantry but also as a vehicle to tell of the exploits of a particular hero – in this case the young Milosh Voyinovich.

[1] TSAR STEFAN DUSHAN THE GREAT (literally 'the Mighty') *(Car Stefan Dušan Silni)* ruled 1331–55, at the height of Serbia's prosperity and power. He was also styled 'the Lawgiver', the codes of law which he introduced being far ahead of those obtaining in most of the rest of mediaeval Europe.

[2] LEDJAN An imaginary name for a 'Latin' town. All foreign Christians who worshipped according to the Roman rite (i.e. in Latin) tended to be lumped together as 'Latins' by the Orthodox Serbs who, of course, worshipped in their own language.

[3] KING MIHAILO *(Kralj Mijailo)* An invented character.

[4] ROKSANDA Tsar Dushan's wife was in fact Yelena *(Jelena)*, but it was customary to call a Tsaritsa by the name of Alexander the Great's wife.

[5] VEZIR Vizier, Chief Minister.

[6] VOYINOVICH *(Vojinović or Voinović)* The patronymic of the sons of Voyin (or Voin), who was Tsar Dushan's Treasurer and who married the Tsar's sister.

[7] PRIZREN Tsar Dushan's capital, in south-western Serbia.

[8] VUCHITERN *(Vučitrn)* A town in the Kosovo region (see note [9] below).

[9] KOSOVO A region of south-west Serbia.

[10] MILOSH (Miloš) The youngest of the three brothers Voyinovich (see note [6] above), Milosh Voyinovich became a legendary hero of the ballads. He is to be distinguished from the other famous hero, Milosh Obilich (see note 3 [4]).

- 213 -

¹¹ SHAR The Shar Mountains *(Šara Planina)* rise out of the Plain of Kosovo.
¹² BULGARIAN A term often used, as here, to mean simply 'shepherd'. The massive, ankle-length woollen coat and the hat which shepherds normally wore were traditionally black. A Balkan audience would have relished the absurdity of Milosh's being able to perform the heroic and, indeed, athletic feats later described in this ballad whilst wearing so cumbersome a disguise.
¹³ KARAVLAH Wallachia, now southern Romania.
¹⁴ SKENDERIA *(Skenderija)* A district in northern Albania (then part of the Serbian empire).

2
Saint Peter and his Mother
(Sveti Petar i Majka mu)

This anonymous ballad illustrates the 'music hall' aspect of the bards' repertoire. It was probably extended by improvised verses to poke fun at local personages. It also illustrates the truism that people with a deep religious faith can take a relaxed view of jokes about it.

3
The Building of Ravanitsa
(Zidanje Ravanice)

This is the second of two versions of the story recorded by Vuk Karadžić. The earlier, shorter version was sung by the bard Starac Raško: this more dramatic version was sung by a bard from the Rudnik area whom Karadžić did not name. The scene is set in the last years of the Serbian empire (as embellished by tradition) and the bard lists the names of many of the doomed nobility who appear again in other ballads, as well as some of the monumental achievements of their predecessors. Ravanitsa Church was, in fact, destroyed more than once. It has been reconstructed in modern times.

¹ KRUSHEVATS *(Kruševac)* Lazar's capital on the River Morava, in south Serbia.
² LAZAR HREBELYANOVICH *(Hrebeljanović)* was a Knez, or Prince. He was accorded the title of Tsar as Commander-in-Chief of the combined armies of the various Serbian kings and their allies who assembled in 1389 to fight the Ottoman Turks at the Battle of Kosovo (in which he perished), and he is variously referred to in the Epic Ballads by either

APPENDIX

title. He was later sanctified by the Orthodox Church as Saint Lazar.

[3] VUK BRANKOVICH *(Branković)* See note 5 [7].

[4] MILOSH OBILICH *(Miloš Obilić,* or *Kobilić)* A nobleman who historically distinguished himself at the Battle of Kosovo by killing Sultan Murat, the Turkish Commander-in-Chief, at the cost of his own life.

[5] YUG-BOGDAN *(Jug-Bogdan)* This nobleman (invariably referred to as 'Old' Yug-Bogdan) is unknown to history, but as legendary heroes he and his nine sons, THE BROTHERS YUGOVICH, appear in many ballads, not always in a flattering light (as here). They are, however, all listed as having died bravely at the Battle of Kosovo, which, in Serbian eyes, compensates for any minor defects of character or conduct.

[6] BANOVICH STRAHINYA See note 4 [1].

[7] STEFAN MUSICH See note 6 [2].

[8] VOIVODA *(Vojvoda)* Voivoda literally means Army- or War-Leader, and therefore equates to the title of 'Duke' in its derivative sense. The term could be honorary, or could be used, as here, to mean 'Lord' in a general sense.

[9] KRAL *(Kralj)* A king. There were greater and lesser kings, and some could best be equated to tribal chieftains. A Kral's wife – a Queen – was a Kralyitsa *(Kraljica),* and his son a Kralyevich *(Kraljević).*

[10] MONUMENTS, ETC. Serbia is rich in superb churches, monasteries, and other building works in the Byzantine style of the mediaeval period, many of which are listed here with the names of their founders (not, in every case, accurately).

[11] RESAVA A small river flowing from the east into the River Morava, but here referred to as a district.

[12] RAVANITSA *(Ravanica)* The site is about thirty miles north-east of Krushevats.

[13] KMET A headman: the 'mayor' of a town or district.

[14] KNEZ A prince, or duke.

[15] RADE THE MASTER-BUILDER *(Rade Neimar)* (Pronounced 'Radé') A famous architect who is known to have been responsible for many notable buildings.

[16] BROTHERS YUGOVICH The nine sons of Yug-Bogdan (see note [5] above).

[17] RELYA KRILATITSA *(Relja Krilatica,* or *Krilati)* 'Winged' Relya was a nobleman often mentioned in the ballads. There are two noble 'Relyas' known to history, one of whom *('Hrelja')* was a contemporary of Tsar Lazar, as in this story, and the other one lived and was buried at Raška, near Novi Pazar (see note [18] below) in later times. It is probable that, with the passage of time, the two personalities have become confused, as is not unusual in the epics.

[18] PAZAR The bard is presumably referring to the town of Novi Pazar

SERBIAN EPIC BALLADS

which, being so far to the south, is an unlikely place in the context of this ballad. It is probably because 'Winged' Relya (see note [17] above) is always traditionally linked with Pazar that it is mentioned here.

[19] RAKIA *(Rakija)* Brandy, of the 'schnapps' sort. When distilled from plums it is called slivovitz *(Šljivovica).*

4
Banovich Strahinya (*Banović Strahinja*)

This long ballad was sung to Vuk Karadžić by the elderly bard Starac Milija. One of the greatest of all epic ballads, it is remarkable for its breadth of characterisation and for the spread and balance of the narrative. The events described in it refer to the concentration of the Ottoman armies shortly before the Battle of Kosovo, in which the legendary hero of this ballad perished.

[1] BANOVICH STRAHINYA This nobleman (a 'Ban' – see note [2] below) is variously known as Strahin *(Strahinj)* or Strahinyich Ban *(Strahinjić Ban),* as throughout this ballad. In the others, however, he is always referred to by the name of this ballad.

[2] BAN A nobleman with estates: a civil governor. A Ban might be equated to an Earl (see also note 25 [4] – 'Banovina').

[3] BANSKA *(Banjska)* A small town in the hills north of the Plain of Kosovo.

[4] KRUSHEVATS See note 3 [1].

[5] YUG-BOGDAN AND THE BROTHERS YUGOVICH See note 3 [5].

[6] YEDREN *(Jedren)* Edirne, formerly Adrianople. This town on the River Maritsa, near the (modern) Bulgarian border with Turkey, is where the Ottoman Turks established their capital after their first successful incursion into Europe during the fourteenth century. It remained so for almost a hundred years until the capture of Constantinople. Even after that great city had become, as Istanbul, the new Imperial capital, Edirne remained an important Turkish centre and a favourite resort of the Ottoman Sultans and their courts.

[7] JANISSARIES *(Janjičari)* Regular troops of the Ottoman Sultan's Bodyguard: a highly-paid corps d'elite.

[8] STRAHINYOVA Throughout this ballad the errant lady is called *Strahinjova ljuba* which means 'Strahin's wife' (her Christian name is not mentioned). In the epics this is unexceptional and there is no problem in narrative passages, but it would sound bizarre if translated literally as a form of address with endearments. When this occurs, therefore, I have compromised by simply calling her 'Strahinyova'.

APPENDIX

5
Tsar Lazar and Tsaritsa Militsa (*Car Lazar i Carica Milica*)

This version of a famous ballad was recited to Vuk Karadžić by the great bard Tešan Podrugović. It describes the eve and immediate aftermath of the Battle of Kosovo, illustrating not only the glory but also the tragedy of war, particularly from the point of view of the womenfolk.

[1] TSAR LAZAR See note 3 [2].
[2] KOSOVO Tsaritsa Militsa is speaking of the impending Battle of Kosovo, which was fought on St Vitus' Day, 1389 (15 June, but observed on 28 June by the modern (western) Gregorian calendar) at Kosovo Polye *(Kosovo Polje)* – 'The Field of Blackbirds' – on the central plain of the Kosovo District. The battlefield lies about five miles south-west of the modern town of Priština.
[3] BROTHERS YUGOVICH See note 3 [16].
[4] KRUSHEVATS See note 3 [1]. The town lies about eighty miles north of the battlefield of Kosovo.
[5] YUG-BOGDAN See note 3 [5].
[6] MILOSH THE VOIVODA *(Vojvoda Miloš)* This was Milosh Obilich (see note 3 [4]).
[7] VUK BRANKOVICH *(Vuk Branković)* A nobleman, married to Tsar Lazar's daughter Mara. He fought at the Battle of Kosovo and survived, dying nine years later in 1398. It may be simply because he did survive that he is always portrayed in the ballads as a traitor, but history does not confirm his alleged treachery.
[8] BANOVICH STRAHINYA See note 4 [1].
[9] SITNITSA *(Sitnica)* A small river which runs through the battlefield of Kosovo.

6
Stefan Musich (*Musić Stefan*)

A ballad of the Battle of Kosovo which contains the famous 'Lazar's Curse' (a commination on any Serb who absented himself from the battle). This tale of a nobleman who, with his contingent, arrived too late at the battlefield to be effective may well reflect real events. Throughout this ballad Tsar Lazar is referred to by his original title of 'Knez', or Prince. Modern research suggests that the bard was either the blind woman Živana, or a blind woman bard from Grgurevci in the Srem district of Slavonia.

[1] MAIDAN *(Majdan)* The location of this town is uncertain. If it was Majdanpek, in eastern Serbia, it would have meant a journey of some two

– 217 –

hundred miles to the battlefield of Kosovo, which could well explain the hero's late arrival, despite his best efforts.

[2] STEFAN MUSICH *(Musić Stevan* or *Stefan)* A nobleman known to history as the son of a chieftain called Musa, who was married to Lazar's sister. (The Serbs indifferently transpose the order of a person's surname and Christian name: I have put them in the order most familiar to English-speaking people, with the Christian name first).

[3] LAZAR See note 3 [2].

[4] MURAT The Turkish Sultan and Commander-in-Chief of the Ottoman army.

[5] SITNITSA See note 5 [9].

7
The Maiden of Kosovo (*Kosovka Devojka*)

One of the most famous, as well as the most tragic of all the Epic Ballads, Vuk Karadžić took down this version from a particular blind woman bard from Grgurevci (to be distinguished from other similar bards from the Srem district of Slavonia). As in so many of the Serbian epics, the suffering of the bereaved womenfolk is emphasised alongside the more glamorously masculine aspect of warfare.

[1] LAZAR See note 3 [2].

[2] MILOSH THE VOIVODA This was Milosh Obilich (see note 3 [4]).

8
The Death of the Mother of the Yugovichi
(*Smrt Majke Jugovića*)

This version of a very famous ballad was collected from an unnamed bard and sent to Vuk Karadžić by the Bishop of Karlovac, in the Krajina (see Note 25 [3]). Many ballads about Kosovo and its aftermath contain expressions of concern for the plight of the womenfolk whose husbands and sons had fallen in the battle. In this one a bereaved mother, with great dignity, attempts to resist displaying her grief but eventually succumbs to it. A principal reason for this ballad's renown is the poetic perfection of the original, which barely survives translation.

[1] YUG-BOGDAN AND THE BROTHERS YUGOVICH (See Note 3 [5]) Whilst the noble 'Old' Yug-Bogdan and his nine sons are not known to history they are famous names in the Epics. In the ballads about Kosovo they are always portrayed as having fought and died heroically in battle.

APPENDIX

9
Marko's First Heroic Deed (*Prvo Junaštvo*)

Bard anonymous. This well-known ballad sets the tone for Marko Kralyevich's legendary way of life as a reluctant vassal of the Turks, with a very short temper.

1 MARKO KRALYEVICH *(Marko Kraljević)* The real Marko Kralyevich was a prince, the son of King Vukashin *(Kralj Vukašin)* who was killed at the Battle of the Maritsa River in 1371. His status is implicit in his name, which means 'Son of a King'. After his father's death Marko reigned at Prilep, or Prilip, in southern Serbia as a vassal of the Turks and he died in battle in 1395, in what is now Romania, fighting on the Turkish side. In legend, however, he came to be portrayed as the most famous of all the Serbian national heroes, surviving, apparently, into the sixteenth century, and is renowned as such throughout the Balkans. The tales about him, of which there are hundreds, are in the realm of enchanted artificiality and he might be said to be the Balkan counterpart of King Arthur or Robin Hood – or a combination of both. He epitomises the ambiguous relationship of the Serbs with their Turkish overlords after the conquest – sometimes he fights and slaughters them, sometimes he outwits them or exposes them to ridicule, and sometimes he serves the Sultan, though usually only temporarily and then at an exorbitant fee! He is portrayed strictly as a hero from the end of the Age of Chivalry (although his general character and habits are rather far from those expected of Chaucer's 'parfait gentil knight'). He knows nothing of firearms or gunpowder and he always acts as an individual champion, rather than as a leader of others. To his Christian faith and to his own people he is staunchly faithful: the very idea of committing apostasy to curry favour with the Turks would never have occurred to him.

2 SHARATS *(Šarac)* Marko Kralyevich's legendary dappled horse.
3 YEDREN See Note 4 [6].

10
Marko Drinks Wine During Ramadan
(*Marko Pije uz Ramazan Vino*)

Bard anonymous. In this ballad Marko Kralyevich shows how brazen effrontery may serve to reduce even the greatest Sultan to impotence.

1 'LAWS' These laws, which existed, applied only to the non-Muslim subjects of the Ottoman Empire – the 'rayah' *(raja)* – who were firmly confined to second-class status in these and many other ways (see also

note 30 [1] – 'Common people').
[2] RAMADAN *(Ramazan)* The Muslim month of fasting during daylight.
[3] MARKO KRALYEVICH See note 9 [1].
[4] HADJI *(Hadžija)* A Muslim who has performed the pilgrimage to Mecca.

11
The Ploughing of Marko Kralyevich
(*Oranje Marka Kraljevića*)

A very famous short ballad. Bard anonymous.

[1] MARKO KRALYEVICH See note 9 [1].
[2] YEVROSIMA *(Jevrosima)* Marko's mother's name was in fact Yelena *(Jelena)*, but she is always called Yevrosima in the ballads. As King *(Kralj)* Vukashin's wife and the mother of a prince, she was, of course, a Queen *(Kraljica)* herself.
[3] JANISSARIES See note 4 [7].

12
How Marko went Hunting with the Turks
(*Lov Markov s Turcima*)

Bard anonymous. This ballad illustrates the permanently uneasy relationship between the Serbs whom Marko Kralyevich personifies (in aspiration, at least) and the Turks, even when they attempt to join together for innocent activities such as sport.

[1] MARKO KRALYEVICH See note 9 [1].
[2] YEDREN See note 4 [6].
[3] BÉ AFERIM. A Turkish expression of approval.

13
Marko Kralyevich and Musa the Highwayman
(*Marko Kraljević i Musa Kesedžija*)

This ballad was recited to Vuk Karadžić by the great bard Tešan Podrugović. It is one of those in which Marko Kralyevich is depicted as being willing to serve the Sultan personally, despite having been imprisoned by him for undisclosed reasons. One amongst its many remarkable features is Marko's admission of remorse at having beaten (partly by trickery, with a hint of supernatural intervention) a 'better hero than himself'.

[1] STAMBOL (Istanbul) The Turkish name for Constantinople (Byzantium)

APPENDIX

which finally fell in 1453 and then became the capital of the Ottoman Empire. The Serbs had always called the city 'Tsarigrad' *(Carigrad)* and continued to do so even after the Tsar of its name (the Byzantine Emperor) had been replaced by the Turkish Sultan.

[2] HADJI See note 10 [4].

[3] MARKO KRALYEVICH See note 9 [1].

[4] RAKIA See note 3 [19].

[5] SHARATS Marko Kralyevich's horse (see note 8 [2]). The bard makes no mention of where Sharats had been during Marko's spell in prison, but it would have been unthinkable for Marko to go on an epic adventure without his legendary horse!

[6] 'GUARDIAN ANGEL' The original is *'Vila'*. The 'vilas' are often mentioned in the ballads. They are mythological nature spirits, usually in the form of beautiful young women, born of dew and herbs and living in the mountains, trees, and clouds. They often appear as 'familiars' to the epic heroes – Marko's personal Vila is here addressed as 'blood-sister' *(posestrima)*.

14
Marko Kralyevich and the Eagle
(*Marko Kraljević i Orao*)

This ballad is pure poetic fantasy, showing the less-often-seen tender side of the mythological hero (and of the eagle itself, come to that), set against the horrors of battle and of burning buildings. The ballad was composed by a blind woman bard from Grgurevci, in the Srem district of Slavonia.

[1] MARKO KRALYEVICH See note 9 [1].

[2] 'SPIRIT OF THE HILLS' The original is *'Vila'* – see note 13 [6].

15
How the Turks came to Marko's Slava
(*Turci u Marka na Slavi*)

For the Serbs, the celebration of 'Slava' is one of the most venerable and deep-rooted of their Christian traditions (see note [2] below). The very title of this ballad, therefore, would have aroused a shudder in a Serbian audience during the Turkish occupation. On this occasion Marko Kralyevich manages not only to hold the intruders up to ridicule but also to make a profit out of them at the same time. The ballad is attributed to the famous blind woman bard, Živana.

[1] MARKO KRALYEVICH See note 9 [1]).

– 221 –

² SLAVA Every Serbian family has a Patron Saint's Day in the Orthodox calendar. Its celebration is called 'Slava' and it is the high point of the year from both the religious and the domestic point of view. The family declares 'open house' and always extends the most lavish hospitality that it can afford (and frequently beyond that, going into debt rather than be seen to stint). A principal feature is the strict obligation to offer food and drink to each and every visitor, whether friend or foe, and whether invited or not.

³ YELENA *(Jelena)* Marko's wife. Yela *(Jela)* and Yelitsa *(Jelica)*, names which appear later in this ballad, are often-used diminutive forms.

⁴ OKE *(Oka)* A unit of weight, approximately 2½ pounds. (Strictly, Marko's bludgeon, at sixty-six okes, would have weighed one-and-a-half hundredweight!)

16
The Death of Marko Kralyevich
(Smrt Marka Kraljevića)

The death of the mythological hero was described in this imaginative ballad by the most famous bard of his time, Filip Višnjić.

¹ MARKO KRALYEVICH See note 9(1).

² 'SPIRIT VOICE'. The original is *'Vila'* – see note 13 ⁶.

³ ANDRIA. It is part of the Marko Kraljević legend that he killed his beloved brother Andria *(Andrija* or *Andrijaš)* in a furious quarrel over the ownership of a horse, buried him secretly, and lied to his mother that it had been a hunting accident.

⁴ VILINDAR The monastery of Hilandar, or Hilander, is on Mount Athos, one of the holiest places in Orthodox Christendom. The monastery was built by the Serbian king Stefan Nemanja and his son, Sava, at the end of the twelfth century.

17
How Miyat Tomich became an Outlaw
(Mijat Tomić Odmeće se u Hajduke)

Bard anonymous. This ballad tells a tale of typical events during the period of Turkish occupation. It describes the dispossession of a small Serbian landowner in Bosnia, his flight into outlawry, and his subsequent way of life as a bandit-leader.

¹ DUVNO A small town in the mountains of western Bosnia, some fifty miles inland from the Adriatic seaport of Split.

APPENDIX

[2] MIYAT TOMICH *(Mijat Tomić)*, also known as Tomich Mihovil *(Tomić Mihovil)*, was a famous haiduk, or outlaw (see note [4] below) of the seventeenth century, the subject of many ballads.

[3] KADI The title of a Turkish judge. (Note: 'Zhupanyats' *(Županjac)* cannot be the modern town of Županja, which is in Slavonia, some two hundred miles inland from Duvno).

[4] HAIDUK *(Hajduk)* The haiduks were basically bandits operating in gangs but, as the victims of their robberies were almost invariably the occupying Turks or their apostate Bosnian collaborators, they were generally admired and supported by the population. It would be wrong to imagine that the haiduks were all simply fugitive ruffians. As the Turkish oppression became more intense all manner of ordinary people were driven to becoming outlaws, but to be a true haiduk a man had to display not only courage and hardihood but also willingness to accept the very strict rules of conduct by which they lived in tightly-knit bands (For instance, if a haiduk was killed in a raid, his exact share of any booty was either handed to his relatives or buried with him). Writing about contemporary events in his Serbian Dictionary (*Srpski Rječnik*, Vienna, 1818) Vuk Karadžić comments on this, and on the remarkable steadfastness and defiance invariably shown by those haiduks who had been captured by the Turks and who were about to be impaled alive (as a matter of routine, well into the nineteenth century). He describes how, even when offered their lives in return for conversion to Islam, every one of them would refuse contemptuously.

A haiduk chief rejoiced in the title 'harambasha' *(harambaša)*. I have, with some reluctance, translated it as 'captain'.

[5] VRAN A mountain range overlooking Duvno. The highest point is over 7000 feet above sea level.

[6] 'BESIDE THE SEA'. The Dalmatian coast was part of the Venetian Empire: here were the 'Christian lands' to which the bard refers.

18
Starina Novak and Bold Radivoye
(*Starina Novak i Deli Radivoje*)

Bard anonymous. This ballad of a day in an outlaw's life ends with a moral.

[1] STARINA NOVAK A famous haiduk (see note 17 [4]) of the second half of the sixteenth century. 'Starina' is an honourable appellation for an 'old man' and Novak evidently had a good run as a haiduk, although he was finally betrayed to the Turks, captured, and put to death.

SERBIAN EPIC BALLADS

[2] ROMANIA *(Romanija)* This is not the country of that name, but a range of mountains to the east of Sarayevo (see note 19 [9]) in Bosnia.

[3] RADIVOYE *(Radivoje)* Novak's brother. (Pronounced with four syllables – 'Radivoyé').

19
Starina Novak and Knez Bogosav
(*Starina Novak i Knez Bogosav*)

This ballad was recited to Vuk Karadžić by the great bard Tešan Podrugović (who had himself been an outlaw). In it Starina Novak, originally a small contractor in Serbia, tells how he was driven into outlawry (in Bosnia, where, he implies, the pickings were better).

[1] STARINA NOVAK See note 18 [1].

[2] RADIVOYE Starina Novak's brother. See note 18 [3].

[3] BOSNA The River Bosna, a tributary of the Sava, gives its name to the territory of Bosnia *(Bosna)*.

[4] KNEZ BOGOSAV In context, this is probably a local chieftain. There is no obvious reason why he should be mentioned in the story. All the ballads' titles are, however, fixed by tradition and are not necessarily logical.

[5] HAIDUK See note 17 [4].

[6] SMEDEREVO A town on the River Danube, about thirty miles east of Belgrade. The Serbian king George Brankovich *(Djuradj Branković)*, who reigned 1427-1456, fortified this and other towns against the Turks, but his wife Yerina *(Jerina)* was popularly blamed for the resulting tax burden and other hardships, apparently for no better reason than that she was a foreigner. (She was in fact Greek, not Turkish, but 'Turk' was the preferred pejorative term).

[7] DRINA The River Drina, a tributary of the Sava, traditionally marked the boundary between Serbia and Bosnia.

[8] ROMANIA See note 18 [2].

[9] SARAYEVO *(Sarajevo)* A 'new town' in eastern Bosnia, built by the Turks on a greenfield site during their occupation and initially populated entirely by Muslims. Being sited on the main strategic and trade route from the east via Serbia, it rapidly became an important commercial centre, with the consequence that the traffic on its approaches was a regular (and evidently profitable) target for the outlaws.

APPENDIX

20
Old Vuyadin (*Stari Vujadin*)

Bard anonymous. The ballad illustrates the importance to the outlaws (as indeed to guerrillas of all sorts) of the practical support of the population and of their reciprocal duty never to betray individual supporters. The reference to overwintering reflects the fact that the outlaws normally only operated from Spring to Autumn, when there was plenty of traffic to intercept: the Balkan winters are so severe that, especially in the days of horses and carts, little could move during them, with the result that banditry became uneconomic. A popular saying indicates that the haiduks' hunting season ran from St George's Day (23 April in the Gregorian calendar) to St Demetrius' Day (26 October).

[1] LIYEVNO *(Lijevno,* now *Livno)* This town in the mountains of western Bosnia was a major Turkish fortress on the frontier with the Venetian Empire. It is on the main road inland from Split, on the Adriatic coast.

[2] HAIDUK See note 17 [4].

21
Mali Radoyitsa (*Mali Radojica*)

Bard anonymous. A typical device of the bards was to open a ballad with a short 'overture' posing dramatic questions in the form of riddles with suggested answers, only to be followed by a contradictory explanation which led into the main story (the so-called 'Slavonic antithesis'). This ballad has such an opening. The rest of it is a good straightforward 'thriller'.

[1] MALI RADOYITSA *(Mali Radojica)* 'Mali' means 'little' and 'Radoyitsa' is a diminutive form of a number of names, *'Radoslav'* and *'Radivoj'* amongst them, all based on the name *'Rade'* (pronounced Radé). 'Little Rade' was a famous haiduk (see note 17 [4]) and was in all probability a very big, strong man, as his exploits in this ballad suggest, his nickname being comparable to that of 'Little John' in the English legends of Robin Hood.

22
The Death of Voivoda Priyezda
(*Smrt Vojvode Prijezde*)

This fine ballad was sung to Vuk Karadžić by the blind woman bard Jeca of Zemun, near Belgrade. It is founded on fact. History relates that in

1413 the Commander of Stalach did refuse to surrender the town to the
Turks and was burned to death in it when the town fell. 'Prijezda',
however, was the name of the Commander at Novo Brdo, one of the last
of the Serbian fortresses to hold out against the Turks: it is possible that
the names had become confused over the centuries.
[1] STALACH *(Stalać)* A small town on the South Morava river (a tributary of
the River Morava itself), about ten miles from Krushevats (see note 3 [1]).
[2] VOIVODA PRIYEZDA *(Vojvoda Prijezda)* As to 'Voivoda', see note 3 [8].
[3] RAKIA See note 3 [19].

23
How the Yakshich Brothers shared their Inheritance
(Dioba Jakšića)

This ballad was written down by Vuk Karadžić from memory of his
father's singing. In mediaeval times a patrimony was normally regarded
as sacrosanct and indivisible, so that even the title of this story has a
special edge – emphasised by the introductory imagery of the Day-star
stopping in its tracks to witness so remarkable a sight as that of two noble
brothers actually sharing their inheritance. It is noteworthy that the story
has the brothers' puerile but deadly quarrel being settled only by the
practical good sense and strength of character of a woman – the elder
brother's wife.
[1] THE YAKSHICH BROTHERS Dimitar Yakshich *(Jakšić Dmitar)* is known
to history as the son of the 15th-century Vojvoda Jakša, and as having
distinguished himself in battle against the Turks after the fall of Serbia.
Nothing is known of a brother called Bogdan, although that name is
attributed to him in this and other epic ballads. Historically Dmitar's
brother's name was Stevan, who is also the subject of some ballads.
[2] KARAVLAH Wallachia. See note 1 [13].
[3] KARABOGDAN Moldavia. Now part of Romania (on the lower Danube).
[4] BANAT A region north-east of Belgrade, across the Danube.
[5] SREM A region west of Belgrade, between the Danube and Sava Rivers.

24
Ailing Doichin *(Bolani Dojčin)*

Bard anonymous. Doichin, or Doichil, of Salonika was a legendary hero
not known to history. This ballad is evidently set at a time before the
Turkish incursions, when Salonika *(Solun)* was still a Serbian town, part
of the Serbian empire, and when the mediaeval concept of settling
important issues by single combat was still in vogue. It emphasises the

APPENDIX

obligations of kinship and the awfulness of betraying them.
[1] VOIVODA See note 3 [8].

25
The Ban of Zrin and the Maiden Begzada
(Ban Zrinjanin i Begzada Djevojka)

Bard anonymous: this ballad is not from Vuk Karadžić's collections. It is remarkable for the pace of the narrative and for the detailed descriptions of the clothing of the Turkish nobility. Throughout the ballad the hero is referred to only as 'The Ban of Zrin' *(Ban Zrinjanin)* never by his actual name. Circumstantial evidence suggests that he was an historical Ban, Knez Nikola Šubić, who held the tenure of Zrin from 1542 to 1566.

[1] BAN A nobleman (see note 4 [2]). Zrin *(Zrinj)* is a frontier town in the Krayina (see note [3] below), about ten miles north of Novi.
[2] NOVI (now Bosanski Novi) A town at the confluence of the rivers Sana and Una, Novi was a frontier fortress of the Ottoman province of Bosnia.
[3] KRAYINA *(Krajina)* Literally 'The Borderland', this is specifically the swathe of territory in the southern part of the Austrian province of Croatia which formed the military border region between the Austrian and the Ottoman Empires. It was populated and defended by Serbs (see Introduction, section one).
[4] BANOVINA The estates and property of a Ban (see note 4 [2]). If a Ban is equated to an Earl, a Banovina would be an Earldom.
[5] OKE See note 15 [4].
[6] JANISSARIES See note 4 [7].
[7] BULYUBASHA *(Buljubaša)* A company commander in the Turkish army.

26
Ivo Senkovich and the Aga of Ribnik
(Ivo Senković i Aga od Ribnika)

This ballad was sung to Vuk Karadžić by the blind woman bard Živana. Throughout most of the period of the Ottoman occupation of the Balkans the Dalmatian littoral and islands remained under the hegemony of Venice (and, in parts, of Austria and Malta), whilst the Turks held the mountains which rise steeply from the narrow coastal strip and, of course, the Bosnian hinterland. Many Serbs and Montenegrins, displaced from their homelands, operated there as irregular border raiders or **'uskoks'** *(uskoci),* who fought against the Turks both by land and sea, often in concert with Austrian or Venetian forces. The uskoks differed from the haiduks (see note 17 [4]) in that they had foreign allies

SERBIAN EPIC BALLADS

and secure bases in territory outside Turkish control from which they could mount their raids and to which they could return. Most tales of the uskoks are of raids and battles (as in, for instance, ballad No 27 – 'Tadia Senyanin'): this one, however, portrays its well-known hero as a champion of an earlier age of chivalry and single combat.

[1] RIBNIK is a small town high in the Dinaric Alps near Gospić, about ten miles inland from the coast as the crow flies, and about forty miles from Senj, but very much farther by the steep and twisting mountain roads.

[2] GEORGE SENKOVICH *(Djurdje Senković)* The name 'Senkovich' or 'Senyanin' *(Senjanin)* simply means 'Man of Senj'. (As to Senj, see note 27 [1]). George was a legendary uskok, the subject of a number of ballads and, in legend, the father of the even more famous uskok Ivo Senkovich (see note [3] below).

[3] IVO SENKOVICH *(Ivo Senković)*, (also known as Ivo Senyanin) was a celebrated uskok, the hero of many epic ballads. His legendary name is probably a pseudonym for a real uskok leader called Ivan Vlatković, who operated out of Senj until his (inevitably violent) death in 1612.

27
Tadia Senyanin (*Senjanin Tadija*)

Bard anonymous. This is a straightforward tale of an adventure of the border raiders ('uskoks' – see note 26), with plenty of action and a surprise ending.

[1] SEN *(Senj)*. Pronounced Señ. A fortified town on the Dalmatian coast, about forty miles south of Rijeka, Senj was, in the 16th and 17th centuries, in Austrian territory and was for many years a major operational base and stronghold of a northern group of uskoks.

[2] TADIA SENYANIN *(Senjanin Tadija)* The popular hero of many ballads, this celebrated uskok is portrayed in legend as a nephew of Ivo Senkovich (see note 26 [3]). 'Tadija' is a common name on the Dalmatian coast and history knows of several uskoks with that name, whilst 'Senyanin' simply means 'of Senj'. One theory is that this particular hero was in fact Tadija Vuković, a famous fighter against the Turks (born c.1690) who came from Sinj, on the River Cetina some twenty miles inland from Split, and that the bards came to confuse the place-names since Senj was so strongly associated with the uskoks.

28
The Three Prisoners (*Tri Sužnja*)

The epic ballads of Montenegro *(Crna Gora)* reflect the character of the

APPENDIX

inhabitants of that harsh and mountainous country: dour, sometimes to the point of grimness, plain, and uncompromising. So implacable and so effective was the unending resistance of the Montenegrins to foreign occupation that the Ottomans took care to isolate that region from the rest of Serbia by creating a buffer zone inhabited entirely by reliable Turks and converts (the Sandžak of Novi Pazar). This ballad describes a typically desperate incident arising out of the refusal of some clans to pay the poll-tax (a recurring theme) and the taking of their chiefs as hostages. There is little embellishment to the tale beyond the gallows humour of the executioner's facetiousness in raising the hopes of two of the prisoners before killing them, and his gullibility (which turns out to be fatal for him). The bard is anonymous.

[1] SKADAR (now Shköder) A town in Albania close to the border with Montenegro.

[2] VUKSAN OF THE ROVCHANI, LIYESH OF THE PIPERI *(Vuksan od Rovaca, Liješ od Pipera)* The Montenegrins are highlanders and have a system of clans very similar to that of the Highland Scots. These prisoners were evidently clan chieftains, as the form of their titles suggests (although they are described as 'Voivodas' – see note 3 [8] – in the original). The Piperi are an ancient and renowned border clan with a ferocious reputation.

[3] KADI See note 17 [3].

[4] HODJA A Muslim priest.

29
How they took Beg Lyubovich's Sheep
(Udar na Ovce Bega Ljubovića)

Bard anonymous. The feuding between Montenegrins and Turks was incessant, bloody, and merciless. Neither side took prisoners except (in rare cases) for ransom, and either side would kill enemy wounded as a matter of course (since, even if maimed, they might still breed). This ballad describes a typical sheep-stealing expedition and skirmish in the terse style of a military report, albeit in the classic poetic form.

[1] PATROL OF FIGHTING MEN The single Serbian word 'cheta' *(četa)* means a military company. Throughout the Ottoman occupation, and throughout Serbia, Montenegro, Bosnia, and Dalmatia, such 'companies' were irregular groups variously bent on harassment of the Turks by destruction, robbery, plunder, or slaughter. The captain of a cheta was called a 'harambasha' *(harambaša)*.

[2] KICHEVO *(Kičevo)* This is not the (modern) Macedonian town of that name, but *Kčevo* (or *Čevo*), a small place in Montenegro about 20 miles north of Cetinje.

SERBIAN EPIC BALLADS

[3] NEVESINYE *(Nevesinje)* (Pronounced Nevesinyé) A hill town well inside Hercegovina about thirty miles east of Mostar and at least fifty miles from the (modern) Montenegrin border.

[4] RUDINE (Pronounced Rudiné) An area on the border between Montenegro and Hercegovina.

[5] NIKSHICH *(Nikšić)* A town in Montenegro at the junction of the main inland routes to Hercegovina.

[6] TURKISH CAPTAINS In the original this second company is called a 'cheta' (see note [1] above), but its leaders are called 'bulyubashas' *(buljubaše)*, which is the Turkish word for a captain. Their names, however, indicate that these two and their band were local converts to Islam and would consequently be regarded as having 'become Turks' *(poturice)*. Although as such they were nominally in league with the Ottoman authorities it seems evident that, in this affair, their aim was not to effect an arrest but rather to get the stolen sheep for themselves, conveniently settling a blood-feud in the process.

30
The Start of the Revolt against the Dahiyas
(Početak Bune protiv Dahija)

This ballad brilliantly illustrates the way in which the bards would present contemporary and recent events, in their role of bringers of news. It describes, in the classic epic form, the beginning of the First Serbian Uprising, which started in February 1804 and was not finally crushed until 1813. It was dictated to Vuk Karadžić by the master-bard Filip Višnjić (who, though blind, had taken a prominent part in it) at the time of the Second Serbian Uprising in 1815. The names of people and places and the events described (albeit with some poetic embellishment) are historically correct, although some of the Serbian chiefs named as dying in the initial Turkish 'purge' were in fact killed later in battle. The long list of names of such leaders who were marked down for slaughter may seem tedious to the modern reader but, of course, would have been of intense interest to a contemporary audience of compatriots. Even some of the ominous meteorological phenomena which are here said to herald the Uprising were in fact recorded at the time in the chronicles.

[1] 'COMMON PEOPLE' There is no simple translation of 'rayah' *(raja)*, which was the term applied to the mass of non-Muslim subjects under Islamic Ottoman rule, since it has a heavy accretion of meaning. It is a contemptuous expression with overtones of oppression, degradation, and poverty. (See also note 10 [1]).

APPENDIX

[2] DAHIYA *(Dahija)* The Dahiyas were Turkish Military Governors in Serbia who, by the beginning of the nineteenth century, were effectively ruling as independent despots, out of the control of their sovereign, the Ottoman Sultan. Historically, this Serbian revolt was not initially aimed at the overthrow of the Sultan's authority, but was specifically a reaction against these local oppressors, who had flagrantly disregarded the Sultan's recent orders to them to improve the lot of his subjects. It turned out to be the first and most significant step in the struggle for complete independence (see Introduction, section one).

[3] TSARIGRAD *(Carigrad)* The speaker refers to the fall of Constantinople on 29 May 1453 and the death in battle within that city of the eighty-sixth and last Byzantine Emperor, Constantine XI Dragases. (See also note 13 [1] – 'Stambol').

[4] MILOSH The speaker refers to Milosh Obilich (see note 3 [4]).

[5] KNEZ See note 3 [14]. *Knez* means 'Prince', but after three centuries of increasingly oppressive Turkish domination, the Serbian title could by now signify little more than chieftain, or 'community leader' in the modern jargon.

[6] KARAGEORGE (*'Crni' Djordje* or *'Karadjordje' Petrović*). 'Kara' means 'black' in Turkish and 'Black George' Petrovich, who lived from 1762 to 1817 was the leader of the First Serbian Uprising. I have used the standard transliteration of his name into English, since he is a well-known figure in modern history and, indeed, the founder of a royal dynasty.

[7] TOPOLA is the small town, about forty miles south of Belgrade, where Karageorge lived and followed the occupation of pig farmer.

[8] OBOR-KNEZ Formerly, a ruling prince: in the historical context of this ballad, a superior chieftain (see note [5] above).

[9] STAMBOL See note 13 [1].

[10] 'FOUR GREAT DAHIYAS' The four Dahiyas named were indeed the perpetrators of the 'purge' of Serbian leaders and were all killed by Karageorge's forces within six months of the start of the Uprising.

[11] ADJI-RUVIM *(Adži-Ruvim)* was an Orthodox priest, an archimandrite. The bard correctly states that he was taken to Belgrade and there murdered, but he probably did not then know of the manner of his death (he was flayed alive by the Turks in an unsuccessful effort to make him give information about the Uprising and its leaders). The Orthodox Church was, throughout the centuries of Turkish occupation, a tower of strength to the Serbs.

[12] DRINA See note 19 [7].

designed by john morgan
typeset in bulmer monotype
cover designed by john besford
printed by progres štampa,
bertranda russella 34a, zemun, yugoslavia
publishing services by akademija nova,
bulevar nikole tesle 3, beograd, yugoslavia